starting and sustaining
a fresh expression of church

Starting and sustaining a fresh expression of church

Share booklets 1-8

Starting and sustaining a fresh expression of church contains Share booklets 1-8, each of which is also available separately.

Further booklets in the series exploring a growing range of other topics are available at <u>freshexpressions.org.uk/share/booklets</u>.

01. how can fresh expressions emerge? — 5
Michael Moynagh with Andy Freeman, Fresh Expressions, 2011, 978-0-9568123-1-5

02. how should we start? — 21
Michael Moynagh with Andy Freeman, Fresh Expressions, 2011, 978-0-9568123-2-2

03. what should we start? — 37
Michael Moynagh with Andy Freeman, Fresh Expressions, 2011, 978-0-9568123-3-9

04. how can we get support? — 53
Michael Moynagh with Andy Freeman, Fresh Expressions, 2011, 978-0-9568123-4-6

05. how can we find our way? 69
Michael Moynagh with Andy Freeman, Fresh Expressions, 2011, 978-0-9568123-4-6

06. how can we be sustainable? 85
Michael Moynagh with Andy Freeman, Fresh Expressions, 2011, 978-0-9568123-4-6

07. how can we be a great team? 101
Michael Moynagh with Andy Freeman, Fresh Expressions, 2011, 978-0-9568123-4-6

08. how can we finance a fresh expression? 117
Michael Moynagh with Andy Freeman, Fresh Expressions, 2011, 978-0-9568123-4-6

how can fresh expressions emerge?

Share booklet 01

This *Share booklet* is one of a series which aims to help you to think about how to start, support and sustain a fresh expression of church.

01 how can fresh expressions emerge?

02 how should we start?

03 what should we start?

04 how can we get support?

05 how can we find our way?

06 how can we be sustainable?

07 how can we be a great team?

08 how can we finance a fresh expression?

09 how can we encourage a fresh expression?

10 how should we teach and preach?

Contents

Go out and stay out	7
A worship-first journey	8
A fresh expressions journey	9
Unpacking *a fresh expressions journey*	12
Moving from 'listening' to 'exploring discipleship'	16

Go out and stay out

Growing a fresh expression of church is not about starting church in a similar culture to our own in order to draw people into the ways of traditional church. Instead it is about incarnational mission, loving and serving people in their own context and 'being' church wherever that may be.

The start of the journey

Society has changed at a dizzying rate in recent years - thanks to a major shift in cultural attitudes and the ways in which we communicate with each other.

What was once the 'norm' has become an exception, including any involvement with Christianity. Today nearly 60% of the UK population finds it almost impossible to connect with church as we usually know it.

Many Christians are now tackling that challenge by developing fresh expressions of church to go out to where people are - and stay there.

But how might a fresh expression emerge? This booklet will help you to think about how the fresh expressions journey can start.

Two possible frameworks

New churches come to birth in many different ways. There is no 'right' approach.

Let us take a look at two contrasting frameworks to help pioneering teams discuss what sort of approach they might be called to and where they might be in the process of starting a new church. We recognise that there are - and will be - many variations from the pathways presented.

The first is **a worship-first journey**, which over the years quite a few churches have adopted, sometimes with fruitful results.

For the 'scarcely' or 'never churched' in particular a different tack may be required, something which we call **a fresh expressions journey**.

A worship-first journey

A large team or congregation is planted, often in a church building threatened with closure. The church plant offers worship and/or preaching as a shop window and members invite their friends to give it a go.

Rapid results?

A variety of events, such as presentations and discussions on contemporary issues, encourage these friends to explore the faith and attend an Alpha, Christianity Explored or Emmaus-type course, where they make a commitment. As a result they join a small group and get more involved in the church's life.

new congregation → **events or course** → **small group or deepening involvement**

The great advantage is that the planting team can scale up quickly. In some versions, a large church might send out a congregation of around 50 with two or three paid staff.

As the congregation grows, it rapidly assumes financial responsibility for the staff and adds to their number. The mission of the new church expands on a self-sustaining basis.

This appears to work especially among people with some church background who have stopped attending and where members of the new congregation have good networks and are using them. But it is less effective in reaching people outside those networks who have difficulty in identifying with the congregation's culture, especially if they have little or no Christian experience. One pioneer who unsuccessfully tried a worship-first approach among young people with hardly any church background later remarked, 'Why would they come?'

In some contexts the two might be combined. A worship-first journey might give birth to a sizeable congregation, which in time asks 'Whom have we not reached?' A fresh expressions journey could then be used to connect with those who are not coming to the new church.

---

 expressions: making a difference DVD
Fresh Expressions, 2011,
978-095600054-5
Chapter 11: King's Cross Church

A London church planted a new congregation into King's Cross.

Chapter 25: 3.08 @ Kingshill

3:08 @ Kingshill is an example of a worship-first church plant that failed to attract those outside the church in significant numbers.

A fresh expressions journey

This starts with listening to God and to the people the pioneering team feels called to serve. The team begins to build loving relationships and engage in acts of service, as Jesus did.

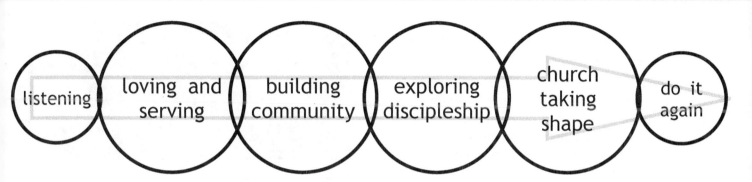

underpinned by prayer, ongoing listening and relationship with the wider church

Framework of trust

Loving relationships and acts of service might range from a spirituality-at-work group, to hanging out with friends, to a 'Saga group' for the over 50s.

Community develops as members of a drop-in centre, an environmental campaigning group or a discussion-over-curry group get to know each other, trust one another and develop a sense of belonging.

'Building community' is valuable in its own right. It is what Jesus did as he ate meals with his followers, travelled with them and devoted periods of special time to them. But it is also important for mission. Loving relationships reveal something of Christ, they give people a partial (though important) experience of church and they create a framework of trust within which to share the Gospel.

Low-key evangelism may continue throughout the initial 'stages', but as the need arises more intentional opportunities will be provided to explore becoming a disciple of Jesus. These could include mentoring individuals on a one-to-one basis. One person may be followed by another, till there is a sufficient number to form a small cell.

Or there could be enough people to form an explorers' group. The pioneering team might use or adapt a published course, or develop its own material. Or it might follow the example of one person who invited her friends to explore spirituality: 'Jesus is known as one of the world's greatest spiritual teachers. Why don't we look at the stories he told and see if we agree with them?'

Some people may come to faith quickly, but for others it will be very gradual. Patiently fanning the fire of the Spirit is a key task for the pioneering team. Once individuals start to believe, they should be encouraged to see discipleship as a life-long process affecting the whole of their lives.

As people begin to enter faith, they will consider what it would mean for them to be church in their culture. Church shaped by the gospel and their culture will emerge round them.

Emerging cells may cluster together in monthly or occasional meetings to provide a larger experience of church. Some will strengthen the spiritual life of the original group from which they came so that the group as a whole becomes more like church.

An Alpha cell might take responsibility for future Alpha courses, designed for people in the wider group. A luncheon club, influenced by a group of new Christians, might incorporate Holy Communion from time to time.

What is church?

Church is what happens when people encounter the risen Lord. At its heart are four sets of relationships:

- **UP relationships with the holy Trinity;**
- **OUT relationships in serving the world;**
- **IN relationships of deepening fellowship within the gathering;**
- **OF relationships in being part of the whole body of Christ.**

Though more is involved, we see church whenever we see these four sets of relationships forming around Christ, who is revealed in Scripture and celebrated in the sacraments.

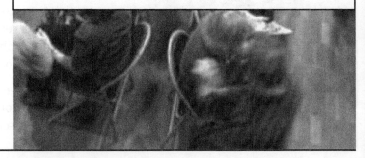

As church takes shape, it will reach out to and serve its context. One of its fruits will be to reproduce itself - to 'do it again' in a style that fits the context is a vital part of what it means to be church.

While the team may have seen this as church from the beginning, those being drawn into faith will grow only gradually in their understanding of themselves as being church. Leaders in the denomination may encourage and support the embryonic church from the beginning, but properly delay permanent recognition till there is evidence of stability.

The Sunday Sanctuary

Story

In 2009, St Luke's, Somerstown, felt that it wasn't reaching the people of their area in Portsmouth. At that time there were about 20 people in the congregation.

Vicar Mark Rodel put forward a proposal to the PCC for the church to move out and relocate to a community room in the Wilmcote House housing block. St Luke's would become The Sunday Sanctuary. It met with a mixed reaction but the proposal was approved. They did not set out to have a worship-first journey by creating a church service in a new setting, but started on the fresh expressions journey in order to meet new people, make friends and share stories.

The initial idea was to have something akin to a 'drop-in' for a couple of hours during which time breakfast would be available. Since then it has become more structured and focuses on engaging with a Bible story. There is no sung worship as such though time is set aside for praying in creative ways.

The move involved a lot of commitment in time, resources and energy from the congregation but they have already doubled the number of people that attended the original St Luke's. The Sunday Sanctuary is still in the process of building and deepening community life but members are beginning to explore discipleship in terms of what they do together. The original community - and the newer members - see themselves as all being evangelised by this process, reshaped by the gospel as they encounter it in new ways and with new people.

Unpacking *a fresh expressions journey*

The journey describes not how individuals find Christ, nor how the internal life of the pioneering team might evolve, but the action the team takes to enable a new expression of church to emerge.

Moving to the middle

The journey is the process encouraged by the team to help people move from the edge of the circle in the diagram to the centre. Whether the team is two or three people or larger, the internal and public aspects of the team's life are different.

The internal dimension is about what the team does to prepare for and bring to birth a new expression of church. Like conception, what is within the team - the church in embryo - will grow into the whole. The spiritual life of the team will shape the fresh expression as it develops. That is one reason why team relationships should be a priority.

The public aspect of the team's life, which is the journey, is about what prayerfully results as the team engages in mission.

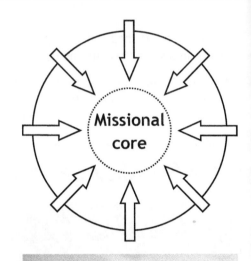

The journey is a sequence of overlapping circles. Overlapping is important because it conveys something of the messiness of real life. 'Loving and serving' and 'building community', for example, may be so tied up together that they happen almost at the same time. Though simultaneous, they nevertheless may be distinct processes.

 How can we be a great team?
(Share booklet 07)
Michael Moynagh, Andy Freeman, Fresh Expressions, 2011, 978-095681237-7

A language cafe may serve afternoon tea and encourage women from immigrant families to learn English by giving them topics to talk about at their tables. This is 'loving and serving'. 'Community' might be encouraged by suggesting that the women sit at the same tables for a few weeks so that they can get to know each other.

As each circle of the journey (page 9) kicks in, it remains present throughout the journey - 'loving and serving' don't stop. But the focus shifts from one circle to the next as the journey develops. The journey may be travelled quickly, but will often take a few years.

> **The Challenge of Change**
> Phil Potter, BRF, 2009,
> 978-184101604-7
>
> **Fresh Expressions in the Urban Context**
> Eleanor Williams, Lulu, 2007, 978-184799213-0
>
> **Mixed Up Blessing: A New Encounter with Being Church**
> Barbara Glasson, Inspire, 2006,
> 978-185852305-7

Some pioneers use different language or the four circles. Phil Potter, an experienced pioneer in Liverpool, encourages lay Christians:

> *...to share your passion, share your life, share your faith, share their journey.*
> **Phil Potter**, The Challenge of Change, *BRF, 2001, p104*

In her study of urban fresh expressions, Eleanor Williams suggests a sequence of blessing, belonging, believing, behaving. If we replace behaving with 'being church', this would map well on to our succession of circles.

Barbara Glasson's account of her experiences in *Mixed-up Blessing* is a good Methodist example of what we describe. She began by walking the streets of central Liverpool for a year, watching and listening. With a group of friends she began baking bread, giving the loaves away. Others began to join this loving and serving core. As they made the bread, community began to form.

> *Side-by-side encounters are infinitely less threatening than face to face ones.*
> **Barbara Glasson**, Mixed-up Blessing, *Inspire, 2006, p39*

In the middle of the day a period of quiet reflection was held in a side room. A Bible passage might be read and people were invited to comment, but not interrupt each other. There was space for silent prayer and reflection. Here was an opportunity for people to explore the Christian faith if they wished. Church gradually took shape.

We can discern a similar journey in the ministry of Jesus. Luke shows him teaching, healing and performing exorcisms in the early part of his public ministry. Then, while this loving and serving continues, there is a new focus on the call of the disciples (Luke 5.1-11, 6.12-16). Jesus is forming community, he describes his followers as his family (Luke 8.19-21). Building community presumably persists alongside his public ministry, but the focus falls more heavily on the process of making disciples - for example, sending out the 12 and 72, and the last supper. Luke describes how church takes shape in his second volume, the Acts of the Apostles.

We don't want to push this sequence too far. Not all fresh expressions grow in this way, especially among the scarcely or never-churched - the Spirit cannot be boxed into a single model. There will be times when the circles are taken in a different order or perhaps get missed out altogether. A fresh expressions journey is therefore both a simplification and a generalisation. You may ask how it fits your experience - might you adapt it or develop an alternative to describe what you are prayerfully expecting to do?

Sometimes, if you peer beneath an apparent exception to the journey, you will find that the journey's sequence is secretly at work. Some university students, for instance, may decide to run Alpha as an apologetics course. They might seem to be starting with exploring discipleship, but look closer. By starting with listening and prayer, they may have discerned that this was the best way, in their situation, to love and serve their fellow students.

Maybe they redouble their efforts to be good and generous friends to their peers. They want Alpha to spring out of a network of loving relationships and their invitations to get a favourable response. Though Christian apologetics is certainly present, during the first evening or two the focus is on building community - through the welcome, the meal, the discussion and much else. The hosts want people to feel at home and come back. Later, although the community dimension remains, attention shifts to encouraging individuals to explore discipleship and make a response. A follow-up course might be the context in which church begins to take shape.

Recognising this (or some other) journey can help you to be more intentional about it. You may be doing some things like building community intuitively. But seeing this as part of an overall process may encourage you to give it particular attention - and ask, 'could we do more to strengthen community?'

St Laurence, Reading

St Laurence, Reading is a church with a mission focus on young people that was started in 2001 and provides a good example of *a fresh expressions journey*. It came into being after leaders started to listen to students at local schools, hearing about their concerns and ideas.

By 2010 it had nearly 50 young people growing in the Christian faith, few with any previous church experience.

But this is far from an 'overnight' success story. A key moment for the church was when the local bishop, Stephen Cottrell, suggested a framework for thinking about what they were doing. Chris Russell and his fellow leaders had been doing more and more things to make contact with young people, and had some great relationships. But in terms of young people coming to faith the fruit was hard to come by; they were seeing hardly any teenagers take definite steps in following Jesus.

Bishop Stephen's framework (right) helped the leaders to become more intentional about what they were doing.

Make contact involves building relationships and engaging in simple acts of service. **Nurture** has building community at its heart. A variety of clubs attract teenagers not mainly through activities but because the young people want to belong. As they enter the faith and **grow in their commitment**, church takes shape around them.

Make contact
e.g. school assemblies, detached youth work

Nurture
e.g. through clubs

Encourage commitment to Jesus
e.g. through special weekends

Grow commitment
e.g. worship

This structure has encouraged the leaders to ask of any activity, 'What happens next?' and to consider whether any of the steps from one 'stage' to the next is too big. For example, they are planning a 'Nurture 2' to turn the leap from 'Nurture' to 'Encourage commitment' into two shorter steps. Far from being a constraint, the framework has helped them stay creative but in a strategic manner.

15

Moving from 'listening' to 'exploring discipleship'

You may see clearly how to 'love and serve' and 'build community' but how do you encourage people to dig deeper and find out more about what it means to be a disciple in today's society? Appropriate evangelism is the answer. Understood in a broad way, it can be a vehicle for the Spirit to travel with people through the circles.

Acts of kindness can be especially powerful.

If people are to see Jesus, they must see his heart of love, which is best shown through generous relationships.

A lads and dads football team might support a lone parent family in their area. A book club with a spiritual dimension might provide financial support for a school library in Uganda.

Many people struggle to be as good as they want to be. Belonging to a group that has an altruistic dimension may help them achieve some of the goodness they aspire to.

As their hearts are warmed by being associated with something good, they may become more committed to the group and be more open to exploring what it means to follow Christ.

 expressions: making a difference
Fresh Expressions, 2011,
978-095600054-5
Chapter 09: Grafted

Grafted shows real kindness and practical support at their weekly drop-in centre.

God talk is about sharing your faith naturally in ordinary conversations and through events that provoke questions about Jesus.

These events may include opportunities for people to hear personal stories about faith. A leisure centre club for women featured talks by people who faced challenging circumstances, such as bereavement or raising a child with a disability. Because the speakers were Christians, they invariably described how God had helped them.

Guests always left with a bunch of flowers. People arriving at the leisure centre often asked, 'Where did you get those?' and were invited to the next meeting!

Missional worship is our phrase for what Ann Morisy calls 'apt liturgy'.

It is designed for people who have little faith or are confused about faith. It provides opportunities for encounters with God that heighten spiritual awareness and encourage individuals to explore Jesus.

Journeying Out: A new approach to Christian mission
Ann Morisy, Continuum, 2006, 978-082648096-5, pp156-64

For instance, leaders of a retired persons' lunch group might put candles on the tables after the plates have been cleared away, play some Christian music, invite someone to read a few verses from the Bible, allow time for silent prayer and ask someone else to read a couple of written prayers - all lasting about 20 minutes. Guests could leave straight after lunch or stay behind for this simple act of worship.

Some church-run cafes have adjacent quiet rooms, perhaps with lighted candles, where individuals can pray and reflect silently. A prayer board played a key role in encouraging women of different ethnicity and backgrounds to talk about spiritual questions. Some who have run Alpha courses among people with little church background testify to the key role of worship. Worship can be quite 'full on' in some contexts if it is led sensitively.

expressions: making a difference
Fresh Expressions, 2011,
978-095600054-5
Chapter 05: CoffeeCraft

CoffeeCraft, in Clee Hill, use a prayer table at their weekly sessions.

As church begins to take shape, missional worship can evolve into a fuller expression of Christian worship.

The experience of healing can play an important part in opening individuals to God.

In a culture that strongly values experience, healing can give people an experience of God. Healing may come through the love of Christian friends, the prayer of Christians (in their personal devotions or corporate worship), healing services or through other kinds of prayer ministry.

Some people have called it power evangelism, while for others it is much more low-key. Avoiding unrealistic expectations is clearly important.

Creative expressions of spirituality can help to increase a group's awareness of spiritual issues.

Members of a group might be invited to express their spiritual longings and understandings through painting, photography, poetry, pottery and in other creative ways.

These might not be explicitly Christian, but frequently they will be pointers to God. As talking points, they may help others to feel more comfortable in expressing their spiritual views and to explore their beliefs.

Conclusion

Throughout the journey it is important to keep listening to God and the people you are serving, and to remain well connected to the wider church. After all, as individuals come into faith they will be baptised into the whole body of Christ.

The pioneering team needs to model this very distinctive Christian identity.

how should we start?

Share booklet 02

This *Share booklet* is one of a series which aims to help you to think about how to start, support and sustain a fresh expression of church.

01 how can fresh expressions emerge?

02 how should we start?

03 what should we start?

04 how can we get support?

05 how can we find our way?

06 how can we be sustainable?

07 how can we be a great team?

08 how can we finance a fresh expression?

09 how can we encourage a fresh expression?

10 how should we teach and preach?

Contents

Where are we heading?	23
A mission heart	24
A mission team	26
Mission values	30
A mission focus	32
Final reflections	34

Where are we heading?

How should we start? is all about a process we call 'exploring'.

Looking for directions

This booklet does not offer you a step-by-step model but it will help you explore what God is doing and where He wants you to be involved. It will also identify important threads - of mission heart, team, values and focus.

As you embark on your journey these ideas may be tangled up with all sorts of other processes. Don't worry. We have found these elements to be important signposts, reminding us that this is God's mission we're involved in. Read on, and as you do, keep asking God what He might be saying to you.

A mission heart

A mission heart is a God-given passion and compassion. This God-given gift will be the spark for joy when lives are changed, the place of tears when people suffer, the seed of hope when things are tough.

Have you got a mission heart?

This deep gift may be one you need to ask for. It may need time to grow but it needs to be there at some stage. Who is the person to be the 'pioneer' of this fresh expression? Maybe God is gifting you in this or calling someone around you. If a church or group of churches is appointing someone to start a fresh expression, the first question may be 'who?'

A mission-hearted person might be:

- **grounded spiritually.**

  We serve as Jesus did, doing only what he saw the Father doing. Personal faith is pioneers' first responsibility.

- **a gatherer of people.**

  They will need to form a team - a 'missional community' - and they will need to help gather people round the community. Paul was a missionary who gathered great teams. Pioneers need the same gift.

- **gifted in leadership.**

  The larger the venture, the greater the leadership skills required. Be prepared to be honest with yourself about the resources you have available.

- **great for the culture.**

  Who or where are you seeking to serve? The person should fit the context, either because they come from a similar culture or because they are gifted in cross-cultural mission.

Think people, not models

If we believe that church must be different we have only half the story. Part of the process of being called to fresh expressions is to let the Holy Spirit complete the story. The Spirit takes you beyond your initial understanding that church must be different to seeing how church can be different for people you are called to serve.

Your imagination expands from 'this is how church could be fresh' to 'this is how it could be fresh for them (or for us)'.

Make the journey

You may not have to abandon your original idea. The Spirit may keep alive your vision but help it to emerge in ways you never expected. But it could be that the Spirit wants your vision to die so that something completely different can come alive. Maybe the Spirit wants to replace your love for an idea with an even greater love for the people you seek to reach.

The key is a dying-to-live attitude

Consider the Good Friday - Easter experience of Jesus. A sacrificial attitude is a gift to be prayed for and nurtured. You could read Philippians 2.5-11 regularly and perhaps even commit it to memory.

A mission team

A mission team (or 'missional community') is vital. In Eden, God's observed 'It is not good that the man should be alone' (Genesis 2.18). This applies as much to growing new churches as to any human activity. It is time to think less about pioneers and more about pioneering teams.

Who will join you?

It's possible that a pioneering venture may have several teams, depending on its size. Imagine a number of concentric circles. At the core may be a small or larger team of leaders whom we call the missional community. Around them may be a number of helpers, possibly comprising several task-based teams. Around them may be the people the venture seeks to serve. Boundaries between the circles should be as porous as possible. This will encourage the venture to be:

- **a partnership between leaders and helpers.**

    We're doing this 'with you' rather than 'for you'.

- **owned.**

    The more people who can help, the more they will have a stake in the venture.

- **sustainable.**

    Tasks will be widely shared, easing the burden on any one person.

Pioneering ministry cannot be done to a community by someone who knows what they need, it can only be done with a community by someone who shares their need.
Angela Shier Jones, Pioneer Ministry and Fresh Expressions of Church, *SPCK, 2009, p123*

Boring Wells

Boring Wells is a network of five mission shaped communities in and around Belfast. Each well has a very different flavour but all share the same vision and values.

The network's name comes from Genesis 26 - the story of Isaac who pursued the vision passed to him by his father, Abraham, of re-opening old wells and digging new ones as sources of life and prosperity for anyone who chose to live close to them.

The team had a sense of continuing the legacy of faith in the Church of Ireland, re-opening wells in old places of faith and digging new wells where there are signs that a new community could be expressed among people distanced from church for whatever reason.

Their exploration as to what God is doing in their area and how they can be involved in it sees them continually trying to be shaped by the mission - and those with whom they are engaging with - rather than predetermining the result.

It took a year to recruit a group of people and initially 35 of them started meeting in a pub but no-one from the local community came to their services and events there. After reading the Mission-shaped Church report they began to consider how church was 'done' and they looked at the possibilities of digging wells that could look like different sorts of things, reflecting the people among whom the well was being dug instead of reflecting what they would like the new church to become.

The wells grew because the mission team had a sense of call in different sorts of areas among certain groups of people rather than being tied to a certain geographical location. The wells each decide how they express church individually but an overarching missional focus feeds a general sense of how the whole family of wells expresses their love of God together.

As well as the network of wells, a network of people has now also developed which is committed to the idea of mission-shaped lives through being a 'family of families'.

> **the sort of people you start with in your missional community may well be the sort of people you end up with in your fresh expression**

Key things to bear in mind when developing a missional community include:

- **the size of the community.**

    There is a no fixed size. Sometimes ventures start with a large core community, maybe including some paid staff. One model is for this core community to draw in people from members' networks so that it grows from perhaps 50 worshippers to around 200. The inflow of new cash and other resources supports the further development of mission and allows quick growth. But growth depends crucially on the community being well-networked to individuals who are open to returning to a lively church with 'their sort of people'. If these conditions are absent, rapid scale-up may not occur and the plant may struggle to sustain its complex model.

    A smaller missional community may be simpler to manage, containing fewer people with pastoral problems and agendas that detract from its mission focus, and members may find it easier to adapt their corporate life to newcomers (fewer people have to agree the changes needed). But scaling up is much harder and takes longer.

    Sometimes it may be possible to combine large and small. A largish planting community would give birth to smaller missional communities contextually attuned to cultures nearby.

expressions: making a difference
Fresh Expressions, 2011,
978-095600054-5
Chapter 16: St George's

St George's are developing missional communities out of a large church.

- **the interests and background of community members.**

    These often determine the sort of fresh expression that emerges. A pioneer who feels called to a specific neighbourhood or network should pray for a missional community with members well connected to the people concerned. One key team member will be a networker - 'a person of peace' (Luke 10.6) who can open doors and draw in people. If the missional community does not have one, pray that God will provide. Remember: the sort of people you start with in your missional community may well be the sort of people you end up with in your fresh expression.

- **considering 'who' before 'what'.**

    Is God bringing you someone with a mission heart, who can be a reliable colleague and who shares your vision for the people you are called to? God may use a person with the right qualities but unsought gifts to take the community in a surprising, yet fruitful direction.

How can we be a great team?
freshexpressions.org.uk/guide/starting/team

Pioneers and missional communities may want to look for colleagues who are:

- **faithful.**
  They are passionate about their faith and inspired by the Great Commission (Matthew 29.19-20).

- **available.**
  They can offer time. Available people know that pioneering can be hard work and discouraging, but despite that they make it a priority.

- **conscientious.**
  They work hard, are reliable, don't let others down and attend carefully to their role in the team. Often they are unsung heroes - 'She always puts out the chairs'.

- **teachable.**
  They are willing to learn from Scripture, tradition, the pioneer context and others in the team.

- **servant-hearted.**
  Willingness to serve the people the community is called to bless is the basis of a mission heart, as we have seen.

expressions: making a difference
Fresh Expressions, 2011,
978-095600054-5
Chapter 01: authentic(?)

authentic(?) took time to develop the right team in Glasgow Harbour.

Starting Mission-Shaped Churches
Stuart P. Robinson, St Paul's Chatswood, 2007, 978-095798321-2, pp42,46

The list on this page is adapted from this book.

It is important to have the courage to say no to someone who asks to join the missional community, or to accept that the group is not right for someone who has joined. This can be especially hard for pioneers who are starting out on their own and perhaps after a year still haven't formed a team. 'Dare I turn down this offer of help?'. Yet the missional community is the human core of the venture. Who is in the community will shape much else. Getting the right team involves the most important decisions you will make.

Turning team into community is an essential task.

The quality of relationships in the missional community will comprise part of the fresh expression's DNA. God exists in relationship and is revealed through healthy human relationships. People are attracted to such relationships in their own right. So forming community is a missional activity.

Mission values

Initial team values are present from the outset and belong to the missional community. They are 'emotional rudders' that guide how the community operates. Members feel strongly about them. These feelings may be based on reason, but these reasons have emotional power and it is this power that gives values their influence.

What values do we feel strongly about?

Agreeing initial values will provide a framework for interpreting the group's experiences. Reality is not simply 'out there', planting itself on our minds. Rather, to a significant extent our minds plant reality on to the world because 'reality' is shaped by our assumptions. Values begin in the interaction between the world out there and our interpretation of it.

Being explicit about the initial team's values will help determine the interpretation members impose on their experiences and observations. Values are the 'whys' and 'hows' of life that members most value.

Values are like an iceberg

Mostly they lie beneath the surface. We take them for granted. They are assumed and unspoken. Making them explicit allows them to be reflected on, even challenged.

The first step in identifying initial team values is to have conversations about what members of the team think is important, perhaps as warm-up activities when it meets.

One possibility might be for members to discuss what a fresh expression of church is and which of the Christian principles that lie behind fresh expressions they most warm to. Both of these topics can be found in the web links above.

You might create a list of important things that people seem to agree with

These might concern:
- how the missional community functions;
- your spiritual boundaries;
- hopes for the fresh expression.

After a while the missional community can begin to look back on its life and ask, 'What has God given to us that seems to be special?' and 'What are the particularly good things about our life together?' These can be the basis for a more stable set of values.

What is a fresh expression of church?
freshexpressions.org.uk/guide/about/whatis

What Christian principles lie behind fresh expressions?
freshexpressions.org.uk/guide/about/principles

It is vital the missional communities do agree some values. It can avoid misunderstanding later and it is better to face fundamental differences at the beginning. If you cannot agree, letting a member of the team go their separate way is no bad thing. Paul and Barnabas parted when they disagreed about the makeup of a mission team (Acts 15.37-40).

safespace

Telford has a reputation as a very secular place. Adult attendance in Anglican churches on Sundays in Telford is 0.64% of the population compared with a national figure of 1.66%.

safespace developed in the town as a way to explore two questions, 'What would a Christian community look like in a culture that was predominantly post church?' and, 'What would it look like if its values were about mission and sharing life with people where they are - as demonstrated in Luke 10 and 1 Thessalonians 2?' The close-knit community numbers around 10-12 on average with people sharing vision for mission and transformation of the town, developing a real sense of it being 'their' place.

They have been described as 'new friars' - coming together as a community, developing a rhythm of life and an intentional spirituality with the focus on 'what difference do we actually make to the place that we find ourselves in and how are we bringing the Kingdom in the town?' Part of the vision for safespace is to be a community reflecting that new monasticism, regularly praying together, growing together and holding each other accountable to their spirituality but being there to serve the place that God has called them to be in.

safespace is exploring things like rhythm of life - how to have an intentional rhythm to daily living and weekly living. They also meet once a week for what is a key 'emotional rudder' in how the community operates; having a meal, breaking bread, sharing wine and spending time in meditation or Scripture and worship. safespace started out with three initial team values of community pilgrimage and mission. These are still the distinctive values of this new monastic community.

A mission focus

A mission focus comes from discerning whom you are called to serve. You can't connect with everyone, obviously. The more focused you are, the easier it is to love and serve the people concerned in depth. You can concentrate resources and develop specialist expertise.

Who are we trying to serve and reach out to?

Jesus came to a specific people, Israel, to start a movement that would reach beyond the nation's boundaries. Your hopes for your mission focus might have a similar flavour.

Things to bear in mind might include:

- **finding centres of stability.**

    These could be schools, or community centres serving relatively stable populations. If the population is constantly changing, you may not have time to build community, nor walk with people on a journey to faith.

- **cohesive groups.**

    They might share a common interest or come from a similar background. It will be easier to form community among them, and travel with them into mature faith. All-age fresh expressions, for example, face the challenge of how to disciple children and adults, whose needs are very different.

- **interest groups.**

    Many more groups might form around a common interest if only someone would be the catalyst to do so. Might a team member be that catalyst, inviting others to join in his or her hobby, creating community among them and beginning a fresh expressions journey?

- **marginal groups.**

    Being pragmatic in selecting a mission focus will often make sense - 'This is the easiest group to serve'. But you may want to think carefully about serving marginal groups, where the needs and challenges are greater. Some pioneer teams have set out to serve a particular group, only to end up working with completely different people. God may bring across your path individuals you least expect.

expressions: making a difference
Fresh Expressions, 2011,
978-095600054-5
Chapter 14: Reconnect

Reconnect is seeing growth in missional community through craft.

Is it right or biblical to form congregations made up of the same kind of people?
freshexpressions.org.uk/ask/diversity

If it is not clear whom you are called to serve, you might try:

- **to find 'a person of peace' - a networker.**

    Networkers are people who can open doors to others. Might a networker take you to the people you are called to bless?

- **to provide an activity that brings you into contact with people you might serve.**

    Examples might include a barbecue for the neighbourhood, a big screen to watch a high-profile sports event or a holiday club for children. You might see what opportunities open up as a result.

A helpful question to ask is 'What would be realistic expectations for working with this group?' Praying through these implications will help you and others in support to have a realistic timescale in mind. If the project is going to take a long time and you need financial backing, it is important for funders to have an accurate sense of the time required.

Final reflections

It's important to take some time to pause and spend time with God to consider where you are.

As you pray through issues surrounding your mission heart, mission team, mission values and mission focus, God will show you whether you have a heart for fresh expressions, who else might share your heart, what values might guide you as you work together and whom you should serve.

As these are clarified, the nature of your call will become more apparent.

Zac's Place

Story

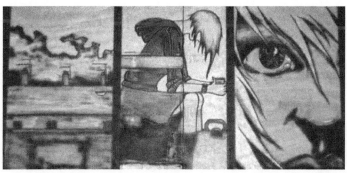

Zac's Place, Swansea, took its name from the story of Zacchaeus and the inspiration of Jesus deliberately choosing to go to the margins of society and keeping company with outcasts.

Its leader, Sean Stillman, had many friends within the biking community. Soon after he had moved to the area, he started to realise there was a need for something a little different to what seemed to be available at that time for them. The bikers were saying, 'We've got a lot of questions, we wanna sit down and talk but there's no way we're going anywhere near a church. How can we do this?' So Zac's Place came about - partly from frustration with not having a viable alternative - but also as a response to people's genuine questions.

Sean had always shied away from setting up an exclusively 'bikers' church' or any other community with a specific 'target audience' because - although he firmly believes that people learn best in peer groups - he also says that mixing everybody together brings a wonderful flavour to the community.

Providing a meal for the people at Zac's Place was one of the first steps on the journey but an important milestone was reached when Sean realised that people were coming together - not just to receive some food or clothing but to share stories with one another.

They then started to voluntarily meet for a Bible study, showing a real desire to learn more about it in what they call their Tribal Gathering. As a 'person of peace', Sean now has a team which continues to provide opportunities for people to participate in saying a prayer, take part in Communion and be baptised.

Sean describes the building of disciples as an 'unbelievably messy process', saying it was difficult to pin down when the transition took place from what many would see as a mission gathering to attracting people in that environment to 'become' church. However, he now looks back to say that Zac's Place has developed, matured and grown into a loving and caring community that wants to serve and follow Jesus.

what should we start?

Share booklet 03

This *Share booklet* is one of a series which aims to help you to think about how to start, support and sustain a fresh expression of church.

01 how can fresh expressions emerge?

02 how should we start?

03 what should we start?

04 how can we get support?

05 how can we find our way?

06 how can we be sustainable?

07 how can we be a great team?

08 how can we finance a fresh expression?

09 how can we encourage a fresh expression?

10 how should we teach and preach?

Contents

A journey of discovery	39
Why listen?	40
Who to listen to?	42
The 'what' of listening	44
The 'how' of listening	46
From listening to doing	50

A journey of discovery

What should we start? is about discernment, a process we call 'discovering'.

Listening to context

This booklet does not offer you a step-by-step model but it will help you find out more about what God is calling you to do by discovering prayerfully what opportunities exist and what resources are available.

Whether the venture is among friends or in a different culture to yours, it's vital that listening to context plays a continuing role in the way the fresh expression develops.

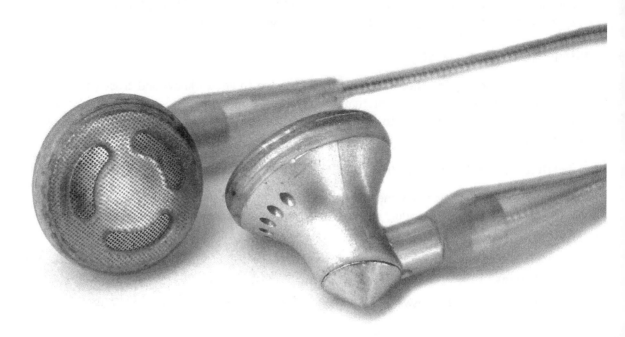

Why listen?

Take time to understand what listening involves because it is absolutely key to the process of discovery throughout the life of your fresh expression.

Listening enables you to discern God's guidance

Remember that mission is firstly God's work not ours. Listening begins with the Holy Spirit speaking to us about how best to love the people we're reaching out to.

Listening is an act of love

The longer you spend listening to people, the more love you will show them. That is why listening is the most important part of growing a fresh expression. Social psychologist Sara Savage says:

 Listen:

(1) to concentrate on hearing something;

(2) to take heed, pay attention.

Collins English Dictionary

The experience of being listened to is so close to the experience of being loved as to be indistinguishable.
Sara Savage, Beta Course, *University of Cambridge, session 2*

Listening builds trust

Spending time attending to others gives them the chance to get to know and trust you. This is the currency that pioneers and their teams trade in. A mutual relationship with the people you are to serve enables you to learn what makes them tick, who's available to help, what works and doesn't. It gives you time to build contacts and form relationships.

Listening is a process Jesus undertook

Read Luke 2.41-52 and notice how the 12-year-old Jesus listened to the Temple authorities in Jerusalem. He entered another culture. He joined an adult culture, the Temple as opposed to the synagogue and Jerusalem rather than Nazareth.

Jesus decided to listen and learn. He established a relationship, sitting respectfully among the religious leaders, meeting them face-to-face. He asked questions (Luke 2.46), the heart of effective listening.

Everyone was amazed at his answers (Luke 2.47). It was a two-way conversation. He took time.

Monk's Road Threshold

Story

The Monk's Road area in Lincoln is very diverse with a scattering of young professionals, elderly people born and brought up in the vicinity and a high population of Poles and other Eastern Europeans. It is also a highly disadvantaged area, suffering from high levels of crime and deprivation.

Leaders of Monk's Road Threshold say that the needs and problems are so varied and wide-ranging that it is all too easy to think, 'Where on earth do we begin? If we try and tackle all of it, there's no way we can.' Instead they started their time in that area with about six months of constant praying because they saw '360 degree listening' or 'listening in the round' as being really important. This listening process helped Threshold to find out how best to love the people they were reaching out to.

They wanted to make sure that community, in a sense of family, underpinned everything that they did. To that end they held quite a few parties, highlighting the fact that the DNA of Monk's Road Threshold was to be welcoming with a heart for building relationships rather than completing tasks.

They had not wanted to be simply another church providing similar things to others. Instead their aim was to engage with people who - for the most part - wouldn't have previous experience of Christianity or experiences of church. Monk's Road Threshold aims to have a more incarnational and relational way of engaging with people and helping them into the kingdom.

Spending time with local residents has brought about mutual trust, relationships and a reminder that they are dealing with 'people, not projects'.

Monk's Road Threshold say, 'If you see planting a new church or engaging in a fresh expression as a strategic agenda...you're doomed from the start. This is God's initiative, it's about his kingdom and all he wants us to do is be faithful and obedient... it's a long-term process.'

Who to listen to

It's time to get your bearings from all four points of the compass and listen 'in the round', identifying your current position and planning where to go next.

Listening to God through Bible study and prayer

Our God is a three-in-one relational God. We build our relationship with him through the Bible and prayer, and as we seek him he speaks to us about our plans.

Listening to the people you are called to serve.

Who are you aiming to reach? You may know this group well. Even so, listening will involve discovering more about their lives.

If you are called to people you know less well some new relationships may have to be made. Start by discovering the people around you and meet:

- **networkers.**

    People who have lots of contacts ('person of peace' in Luke 10.6). They will tell you about their networks and put you in touch with others.

- **agencies.**

    Those providing services in your neighbourhood. These could be head teachers, police or health visitors.

- **businesses.**

    For example, the corner shop or hairdresser. They will know your area well.

Remember that listening is about establishing a relationship. It's not a one-way process. So ask yourself, 'If Jesus is already present in the people we are called to serve, how might they be a blessing to us?'

Listening should open the door to mutual relationships.

Bible study and pray

The wider church

 expressions: making a difference
Fresh Expressions, 2011,
978-095600054-5
Chapter 01: authentic(?)

The missional team at authentic(?) extensively listened and researched in the first few months.

DVD

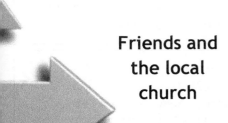

Friends and the local church

e people you feel called to serve

Listening to friends and the local church

This is easily forgotten, but is a vital part of the discovering process. Who are you acting on behalf of? Has anyone authorised what you're doing? Spend time sharing with them as you learn and your ideas evolve.

Ask the local church and/or your friends for prayer support. God may speak through them to help your discernment. So keep them up to date with what you are discovering and seek their reactions.

Don't forget that people praying may be a source of time, wisdom, knowledge, skills or money as your venture develops. Listening intently to them at every stage will help to engage them and get their commitment.

Some pioneers find that one of their biggest headaches is their relationships with the local church. They encounter misunderstanding, unrealistic expectations and often suspicion. Managing these responses is helped by explaining constantly what you are doing, attending to the reaction and then showing that you have listened. Trust grows when people feel that they have been understood. Listening builds up the body of Christ.

Listening to the wider church

The Church at large provides a library of wisdom and experience. Start talking with other pioneers. No context is the same, but the experience of others can enthuse you, spark thoughts, give you confidence, illustrate good practice and alert you to pitfalls.

Christianity Rediscovered
Vincent J. Donovan, SCM Press, 2001, 978-033402855-0

Start exploring the stories of church planting in other traditions, contexts and times. What can be learnt from church planting in Africa or from the 18th century Wesley revival? How about contemporary resources for church planting? You may find all sorts of ideas.

The 'what' of listening

Are you starting with a blank canvas for your fresh expression or do you feel called to a specific vision? You need to know what you should be listening for.

'Testing' times

Allow other people's ideas and visions to interact with your hopes for the fresh expression. Maybe you have a clear idea of what your new church will be like. Be willing to test these thoughts against others' ideas and see what emerges. Prayerful vision can take time to develop.

In Share➔ *How should we start* (Share booklet 02) we suggested that normally one's prime calling should be to serve a group of people rather than to follow a single model of fresh expressions.

However you may feel called to, and be equipped for a specific type of ministry and have a vision for it. In which case listening will be about whether this particular context is the best situation in which to pursue your vision and if so, how your vision should be adapted to it.

Be careful about ownership here. Does everyone share the vision and want to shape it? Be prepared to give concepts away and encourage new ideas.

Or maybe your missional community is starting with a blank piece of paper and has no idea how to serve the people it is called to. It will be asking, 'How can we best serve these people with the resources we've got?' To answer that, besides realism about the support you can draw on, you will need a deep understanding of the people concerned, their culture, spirituality and attitudes.

---

expressions: making a difference DVD
Fresh Expressions, 2011,
978-095600054-5
Chapter 06: Colin Brown

Colin Brown takes time get to know people before rushing to start a new church for the artistic community of Falmouth.

How should we start BOOK
(Share booklet 02)
Michael Moynagh, Andy Freeman, Fresh Expressions, 2011, 978-095681232-2

Begin by asking what you already know. Even if your 'mission focus' comprises people you don't know well, you may be surprised by the amount of knowledge you missional community already has.

Then begin to fill the gaps. Ask questions about the environment and people around you. We'd suggest the following, but why not add your own?

Helpful questions to ask might include:
- **what do people's lives look like?**
- **what do people value?**
- **who is most effectively solving problems faced by these people, and why?**

    You may have to find out what is going on elsewhere.

- **what problems aren't being addressed?**
- **who are the key networkers?**
- **how might these people connect with the Gospel?**

    What would challenge them? What do they think about church, God and spirituality? Do they pray?

- **what resources might be available?**

As you listen, keep notes of what you hear. A record can be used in the group's prayers and to inform praying friends or the church.

The 'how' of listening

Consider some methods of listening.

In *Planting Churches*, author Stuart Murray suggests some ways of listening which we have expanded here.

>
> **Planting Churches: A Framework for Practitioners**
> Stuart Murray, Paternoster, 2008,
> 978-184227611-2, pp86-94

Experimentation

Experiments involve learning by doing. You might open a stall in a farmer's market and give the other stall-holders free refreshments during the day. As you chat to customers, ideas might form, possibly a 'welcome lunch' in the local café with a discussion about spirituality. You give it a try - a second experiment. In time you might offer a Christianity discovery course, and this becomes a third experiment. If an experiment doesn't work try something else.

You can't learn everything before you do anything - you'd never get started. Effective pioneers often do only enough research to justify the next step. They proceed by research, action, more research and then more action.

>
> **expressions: making a difference**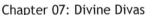
> Fresh Expressions, 2011,
> 978-095600054-5
> Chapter 07: Divine Divas
>
> Divine Divas experiments with a number of activities and events in order to engage with those who would never go to Sunday church.

Participation

Joining in may be a simple early step. As you get to know people, you may begin to take part in their activities and immerse yourself in their lives, like Jesus did. What about volunteering for the social committee at work, or the residents' association or a school governing body?

Participation can make you dependent in some way on the people you seek to serve. The 72 sent out by Jesus were to take nothing with them (Luke 10.4). They were to rely utterly on the hospitality of the village they entered. This dependence would have drawn them into the village's life as they were fed, given shelter and made welcome.

When you make yourself dependent, you give the other person permission to include you in their life. This is an important step to identifying with them. So don't only offer help, ask for help.

Conversation

Get talking! This simple step allows you to listen to people's stories, ask probing but non-intrusive questions and develop mutually enriching relationships. What about a questionnaire, a focus group or a series of interviews? These can all be ways of starting a conversation. Or simply hang out with people.

If you are engaged in listening in the round, conversations will include people who are praying for you or the church leaders to whom you are accountable and perhaps people in the wider church who have wisdom or experience to share.

Observation

Look while you listen. It can tell you a great deal about the neighbourhood or network - what people do, where they gather, what they value, who relates to whom and lots more.

Before starting her now famous 'bread church', Methodist minister Barbara Glasson spent a whole year walking the streets of central Liverpool at all times of the day and night, observing the city's rhythms of life. She discovered some of the places where God was ahead of her.

Mixed Up Blessing: A New Encounter with Being Church
Barbara Glasson, Inspire, 2006, 978-185852305-7, pp1-34

Observation may include walking round the area alone or with others in the team, at different times of day and night, perhaps praying as you go. You might spend a day in a local community project, watching how things are done.

Stuart Murray writes:

Being attentive to what is known as "spatial symbolism" is important - discerning the historical, cultural and spiritual messages conveyed by buildings and locations...
Stuart Murray, Planting Churches, *Paternoster, 2008, p88*

Investigation

This involves researching relevant issues in more depth. It includes finding out more about the people you are called to serve, and also learning from the experience of the wider church. You might want to read some books about contextual church planting, such as the ones referred to in this booklet.

Your investigations could include looking at other fresh expressions of church by:

- watching some of the DVDs published by Fresh Expressions;
- attending a Fresh Expressions *vision day* to hear stories of what others have done;
- reading stories in Church Army's ***Encounters on the Edge*** series;
- visiting a fresh expression, perhaps in a similar mission context to yours.

Don't forget to investigate the culture around you. If you are thinking of beginning a church in a geographical community, you might visit council offices, the local library and websites to learn more about demographic trends, building development plans, social needs, employment patterns or local history.

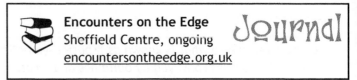

Encounters on the Edge
Sheffield Centre, ongoing
encountersontheedge.org.uk
Journal

To avoid being swamped by too much information, it is wise to focus on key issues that have emerged from the other modes of listening.

Imagination

Letting your creative side loose will help you to process all that you are learning from these different forms of discovery. Imagination allows you to be as off-the-wall as you like - 'what would happen if...?' You may come up with a brainwave. If an idea lingers, you can test it on other people.

Imagination is the reflective part of listening, whereas all the other methods - from 'experimentation' to 'investigation' - entail doing something.

authentic(?)

Story

The influx of thousands of people into a docklands regeneration project in Glasgow prompted a call to think about new ways of doing church. As a result, the Glasgow Harbour initiative - known as authentic(?) - was set up by churches in the area.

The authentic(?) team started by asking themselves the question, 'What does living out God's kingdom look like for the people here?' The 'how' of listening led them to observe and investigate their surroundings through an 18-month mission audit - not only to understand the culture of individuals moving in but also what their homes, cars, and the type of local shops being built said about them.

The audit firstly focused on qualitative data which included the team 'hanging around' the area itself to try and ascertain who the residents were, what kind of culture they came from, what hours they kept and where they worked.

The second, quantitative, aspect was a much more book based analysis. The team looked at old Ordnance Survey Maps of the area, researched history books as to previous land ownership to glean how it had changed over many years and to see where they could go in the future - to find what they described as the 'keys to the Gospel'.'

One of the key questions for them was 'how do we take the mission audit's conclusions and turn them into a positive reality?' A hankering for community was identified as important but the design of the buildings, with many security features for residents, actually inhibited community - particularly as there were no communal meeting places in the development.

Some members of the authentic(?) team moved into a flat in the harbour to have a place on site where people could be invited for a meal and generally practice hospitality. They continue to explore ways in which they can gather people together, including the launch of the authentic(?) curry house and the development of a greater internet presence in order to promote online community.

From listening to doing

Bringing everything together.

What happens now?

You will need to draw conclusions about what you are learning and prayerfully consider what God is calling you to do. Martin Robinson suggests that four helpful questions could be:

- what's going on here?
- what shall we do in response?
- how can we make it happen?
- what will be the result?

Planting Mission-Shaped Churches Today
Martin Robinson, Monarch, 2006, 978-185424728-5, p98

How should we start (Share booklet 02)
Michael Moynagh, Andy Freeman, Fresh Expressions, 2011, 978-095681232-2

Don't forget to share your emerging thoughts with others. Take time to talk to the people you seek to serve. Are they beginning to own the vision? Share with those to whom you are accountable, who have given advice and have been praying for you. Do they think you are on the right track - that you are hearing God's call?

Do you and your missional community have a sense of inner peace and gentle encouragement from God? Are your ideas practical and can you imagine God working through them?

The result of the discovering process will be a vision for how you can respond to your shared call, described in 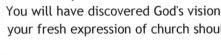 How should we start (Share booklet 02) and best serve your context with the resources available. You will have discovered God's vision for what shape your fresh expression of church should take.

Discovering leads to shared vision

Be aware that this process may have changed you and others in your missional community.

Take time to assess how listening has affected you and how you are feeling now.

Remember, too, that the discovering process will be far from over. You will need to keep listening at every point of the continuing journey - to the people you are called to serve, to those to whom you are accountable, to the wider church and to God directly in prayer and Bible study.

Through this listening, the Spirit will lead you to the next stage and as your fresh expression unfolds step by step the vision will evolve.

> **How can we get support?** (Share booklet 04)
> **How can we find our way?** (Share booklet 05)
> Michael Moynagh, Andy Freeman, Fresh Expressions, 2011, 978-095681234-6 / 978-095681235-3

The discovering process is unpacked further in Share➜ *How can we get support?* (*Share booklet* 04) and Share➜ *How can we find our way?* (*Share booklet* 05).

how can we get support?

Share booklet 04

This *Share booklet* is one of a series which aims to help you to think about how to start, support and sustain a fresh expression of church.

01 how can fresh expressions emerge?
02 how should we start?
03 what should we start?
04 how can we get support?
05 how can we find our way?
06 how can we be sustainable?
07 how can we be a great team?
08 how can we finance a fresh expression?
09 how can we encourage a fresh expression?
10 how should we teach and preach?

Contents

Finding your way	55
Enlisting support	56
Prayer backing	58
The people you are called to serve	60
People who open doors	62
What's in a name?	66

Finding your way

How can we get support? is about how to check out your ideas and plans with the people whose backing the venture needs.

You'll never walk alone

This booklet does not offer you a step-by-step model but it will help you find out more about the 'thread' which will continue throughout a fresh expression's life.

Fresh expressions of church never begin in isolation. They always need support from outside - prayerfully and practically, from above and beside, to allow and to encourage.

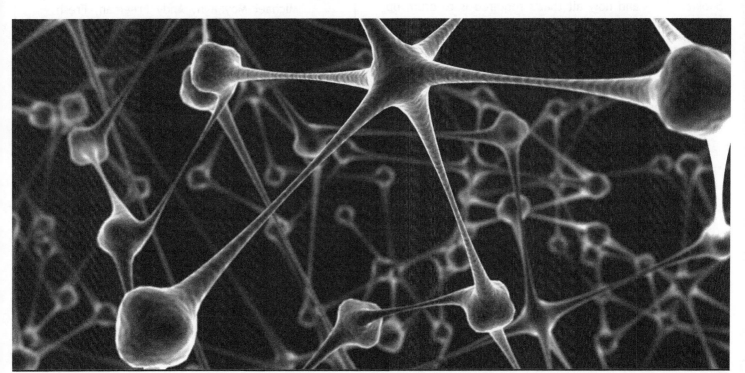

Enlisting support

Everything seems to be in place but how do you win the backing of those outside your community? There are a number of methods but each his its limitations.

Sounding the drum

Securing support and resources will be important for any fresh expression of church, large or small. At the very least, it will include the support of those you feel called to serve. Taking their feedback seriously will be vital to the success of your project. But enlisting support may also entail getting permission, mobilising volunteers, raising money and much more. It can be a major task for the missional community. There are different ways of going about it.

The salesperson model is at one end of the spectrum. It involves making a pitch for support to interested parties. It assumes that the pioneer or missional community knows what should happen. Members have done their discovering, the vision is clear - see Share➜ *What should we start?* (*Share booklet* 03) - and now all that's required is to drum up support.

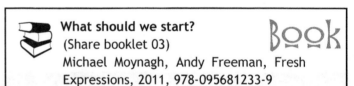

What should we start?
(Share booklet 03)
Michael Moynagh, Andy Freeman, Fresh Expressions, 2011, 978-095681233-9

The model can work well if the leader has a charismatic personality - if they are perceptive, adaptable and can create a positive impression through their communication. But using this model has limitations:

- **not everyone has these attributes in abundance.**

    More reserved leaders may need a different approach. Indeed, if the salesperson's pitch appears to be the only model, less charismatic individuals may be put off starting a venture.

- **the model can be stressful.**

    It sets the leader up for disappointment if the vision does not get the support it needs.

- **the model increases risk.**

    People get swept along by the pioneer's enthusiasm and warning voices are drowned out. However well the missional community has listened to the context, its vision may contain a flaw. Someone outside the team may be aware of a change in circumstances or have an idea that could improve the proposal. This feedback is hard to hear if the pioneer is in selling rather than listening mode.

A testing model, at the other end of the spectrum, involves constantly trying out the missional community's vision and ideas for realising it on potential 'stakeholders' outside the group. 'This is where our thinking has got to. How do you react?'

expressions: making a difference
Fresh Expressions, 2011,
978-095600054-5
Chapter 04: Church for the Night

Church for the Night is slowly evolving based on the feedback received from those it is seeking to serve.

The personal qualities of a charismatic leader will still come into play, but there is room also for less charismatic pioneers.

The missional community gathers support not mainly by selling a concept, but by engaging other people as partners. Persuasion occurs through the 'co-production' of the venture - the team produces the fresh expression with other people.

The process can be slower than 'selling' because the missional community more frequently goes back to potential stakeholders as it forms its ideas. But the advantages are considerable:

- **the community forms stronger relationships with other people.**

  Ownership is gained. Trust, respect and friendliness increase, all of which make support for the venture more probable.

- **the community keeps open to new ideas and alternative solutions.**

  A wider pool of wisdom, knowledge and personal contacts becomes the base of the project.

- **challenges can be viewed in a constructive light.**

  Rather than opposition being viewed negatively, it can be seen as an opportunity for learning. The outcome may be better than the original idea.

Prayer backing

A lot of hard work has gone on behind the scenes and there are a million things on your 'to do' list but take time to have that all-important prayer back-up in place.

'Our Father...'

It's vital not to forget the importance of prayer. Christians at the core of the fresh expression will be praying for it, but their prayers can be helpfully supported by other people.

These partners could be friends, members of your local church or interested parties. Although dispersed, they can be a real asset.

Involving a wider circle of prayer partners:

- **will strengthen the spiritual heart of the venture.**

  Prayer played a key role in Jesus' ministry and in the growth of the early church.

- **will open more channels for God's guidance.**

  There will be more people to pass on insights and wisdom gained through prayer.

- **will expand the potential for practical support.**

  The more people praying for specific help, the more people there may be who know someone who can provide that help.

- **will assist the missional community in remaining connected to the wider church.**

  This will provide a source of sustenance and an expression of their common identity in Christ.

- **will require good communication.**

  Keep telling stories. Keep providing fuel for prayer.

Ashburton Methodist Church

Ashburton Methodist Church had always wanted to live out their discipleship in worship and mission by working through Teignbridge Circuit in partnership with other local churches and a wide range of organisations in the community.

The church is a listed building within Dartmoor National Park. About 50% of the core congregation of 30 are in a more elderly age group with the rest tending to range from 45 to 65.

They got to a point where they knew the church needed to be doing things differently but they didn't quite know how that was to be achieved.

The change started when Plymouth and Exeter District did a Review with them in 2008. One result of this saw 11 members of the church go on the Pioneer Disciple Course - the specially tailored *mission shaped ministry* course in Devon - during the following year.

The thoughts of all of the Ashburton people taking part were stimulated collectively. It was permission-giving as well in that it was deemed OK to take risks and try things. If they didn't work out it wasn't necessarily a failure.

Lots of ideas were then coming to the fore: film evenings, a puppet ministry, book club. People would say, 'This is my particular area of interest, can I try it?' Each time they were told 'Have a go. If nothing else it will give you experience and confidence. Nothing ventured, nothing gained - and see where God leads us.'

Regular activities now include daily prayers from 7.45 to 8.30am, a Christian meditation group and a fortnightly Church Community group time for puddings, prayers and discussion.

They say it feels as if they are at a very early stage but it's a good place to be as they seek to use their interests for the glory of God and serve those around them. Support for this new approach has come about through a testing model which involves constantly trying out the missional community's vision - and ideas for making it happen - on potential 'stakeholders' outside the group.

The people you are called to serve

Obviously your fresh expression must have support among those you're seeking to reach. A 'testing' process here may involve cementing existing relationships. As trust grows, you may be able to encourage people to shape your vision further and how it is to be achieved.

Who are you?

Encouraging volunteers from the mission context will increase commitment to the venture, and volunteers will be likely to invite their friends. In some circumstances, might volunteers contribute to the spiritual dimension of the venture as well as to practical aspects? A community of artists, for example, could have a spiritual zone where they meet. Why shouldn't someone with no obvious faith be asked to populate the zone with books showing religious art?

Sharing leadership will help individuals grow in confidence, be a first step toward making the emerging church self-sustaining and will be an expression of faith that the Spirit has been preparing within the hearts of those involved.

expressions: making a difference
Fresh Expressions, 2011,
978-095600054-5
Chapter 17: Sanctus1 and Nexus

In Sanctus1 and Nexus, a love of art is being used to help individuals engage with spiritual issues.

Good publicity of course will help you to connect with those you want to reach. A clear identity, based on a name, logo and strap line that can be used on all your publicity, will enable people to recognise you.

The **Discovery Days Community Project** near Oxford used the strap line: 'Discover your neighbour, discover your community and discover God.'

Gently making clear that yours is a Christian venture will allow you to develop the spiritual aspect of your work without anyone thinking they were drawn in under false pretences.

Ask what sort of relationship with the audience your publicity is fostering. Does it have an 'us-to-you' feel, for instance, or does it welcome feedback and ideas? Will it encourage ownership? For example, will information about one of your activities be the first time that people hear about you? Or will your first bit of publicity advertise an open meeting, when you will consult people on the possibilities you have in mind?

Word of mouth can often be the best publicity. You will be well on the way if you have the support of one or two people with lots of friends and contacts they can invite. These networkers are the modern equivalents of the 'person of peace' Jesus referred to in Luke 10.6.

If you are thinking of a public launch but haven't found a networker or two, you might ask whether you are ready to start.

St George's

Story

'How are we going to shape a church that can keep on growing and not be dependent on the size of a building or the number of professional leaders?' That was the question facing St George's, Deal, in 2002.

St George's was a busy and popular place but the leaders wanted to create a church that could engage with those who would never set foot in a traditional church building.

Now they have missional communities, or clusters, comprising mission-focused networks of anything from 15 to 60 people.

Mobilising everyone to be missionary disciples has led to the development of a whole variety of diverse networks being reached through these communities. People who previously were sitting in the pews - along the lines of a 'provider-client' type of model - are now doing all kinds of things that they never dreamed they would be doing.

As they've gone out and taken on these new roles with new responsibilities, sharing leadership, the people have discovered the need to depend upon God. As a result they've grown spiritually, in their discipleship and in their confidence.

This has brought about a release of 40 new missional leaders - a real treasure trove of talent and expression of faith.

St George's, Deal, says that one size of 'church' no longer fits all. Instead the need is for something that's flexible, open and in which the seeds of the gospel can grow into the fruit of a church truly following Christ.

Another important new community to evolve has been at the Church Centre. As the centre continues to be an 'attractional model' with newcomers regularly arriving, this central community called 'Shoreline' is able to invite new people into it and give new people time to experience and understand the concept of missional communities before stepping into one that is meeting outside.

People who open doors

Look out for those – both inside and outside the church – who have the power to say 'yes' or 'no' as your fresh expression gets off the ground and gains momentum. Who are they? What can you do to get alongside them and work in tandem?

Permission-givers

Permission-givers play a key role in opening doors and allowing the venture to flourish. They may be outside the church or within. Their support is crucial.

Permission-givers outside the church include anyone whose permission you need to start and develop your fresh expression, such as the management of the community centre you plan to use.

Winning their trust will be helped by relating your ideas to their objectives and priorities. Permission-givers will be on your side if they feel that you are on theirs.

So if you plan a school-based fresh expression, for instance, you may want to frame your ideas in terms of the school's desire to serve the local community. 'Testing' would involve conversations about whether your ideas fit this remit and how they could be shaped to make a greater contribution to it.

Permission-givers within the church will be important, especially if your fresh expression comes out of a local church or group of churches. Those in authority will be concerned about a number of issues, one of which will be accountability.

> **Bishops' Mission Orders**
> freshexpressions.org.uk/guide/supporting/bmo

Think how Jesus felt accountable to his Father and how his Father provided him with support. There is a mutual dimension to accountability, which includes being honest and open together and owning both successes and failures. Low control, high accountability is a great principle.

Within this broad framework, you will need to think through the practical arrangements. Who will leader(s) of the fresh expression be accountable to? How will this accountability be expressed? What are the financial expectations? When and how will review take place? Will someone need to be authorized to preside over Holy Communion? Who else needs to know how the fresh expression is getting on?

The relationship between the fresh expression and its parent church should be made clear from an early stage. The ideal is a culture of provisional recognition that allows the fresh expression to be progressively recognized in a simple way as it becomes more fully church.

If you are in the Church of England and planning to start a fresh expression in another parish, there is some important legislation that came into effect in 2008. The Dioceses, Pastoral and Mission Measure and its Code of Practice make it easier to establish a fresh expression in another parish, even if this is not welcomed by the incumbent and PCC. The Bishop can issue a Bishop's Mission Order (BMO) to establish a new mission initiative that fosters or develops a form of Christian community.

Purse strings

Finance is an enabler of mission when handled well. So particular care should be taken over the financial arrangements for a church-start, especially when a full-time post is being created. A person in the team with basic book-keeping skills will be essential, and someone with accountancy qualifications should be available to give advice.

How can we finance a fresh expression? (Share booklet 08) Book
John Preston, Andrew Roberts, Fresh Expressions, 2011, 978-095681238-4

Developing a sustainable income starts by understanding the distinction between 'capital' (or 'start-up') income and ongoing income (or 'revenue'). The first covers initial one-off costs such as the purchase of equipment, while the second meets ongoing costs such as rent, putting money aside to replace worn-out equipment and salaries.

Depending on the venture, it can take several years to develop revenue to cover ongoing costs. Grant-makers and others who financially support a venture will normally want to restrict the timeframe of their contribution. So it is wise to be thinking well in advance how your initiative will become financially self-supporting.

Ask yourself:
- will the core team and some of their friends be the mainstay of financial support?
- will funding from your parent church (where relevant) be available on an ongoing basis?
- can you develop a network of financial supporters, perhaps starting with your prayer partners?
- can you ask for donations from the people you serve, or introduce a fixed charge?
- as people come into faith, what place will Christian giving play in their discipleship?
- what combination of these streams might be possible?

You should project your expected annual costs and income (both start-up and ongoing) over the medium to long term - perhaps three to five years if you are a large-ish venture. Again depending on size, the same should be done on a month-by-month basis over the next year or two. As circumstances change, you can update your projections.

A simple business plan will be necessary if you are approaching people for money. Include details of your aim, the opportunities you face, the context, the people involved in leading the venture and their expertise and experience, a detailed cost breakdown and your projected financial needs, and any potential risks.

Realism is vital in deciding the size of financial commitment you take on.

You might ask:

- do we expect the venture to become self-financing?
- how long will that take?
- will funders continue to give long term?
- are you confident about alternative sources of finance ? Who?

Addressing these questions may encourage you to opt for a more gradual or simple approach. See Share How can we be sustainable? (Share booklet 06).

How can we be sustainable?
(Share booklet 06)
Michael Moynagh, Andy Freeman, Fresh Expressions, 2011, 978-095681236-0

Measuring results

This will be required by most funders, who will want to evaluate the fruitfulness of their financial support. A 'theology of evaluation' can be developed round the concept of discernment. Evaluating the results of a fresh expression can be a means of discerning whether and how the Spirit has been at work. Learning from this discernment can guide the venture's further development, and if the learning is shared add to the wisdom of the wider church. Three important questions are:

- **how does the venture reflect its aims?**

  What aims are translated into what practices?

- **what outcomes will indicate effectiveness of these practices?**

  Let these include 'hard outcomes', such as the numbers being served by the venture and the number coming into faith, and 'softer outcomes' like the impact on participants' lives and on the community outside.

- **how can these indicators be evaluated?**

  Feedback from those concerned, through a simple questionnaire or a focus group or the enquiries of a 'mystery visitor', might be a possibility.

What's in a name?

How your fresh expression is perceived in the wider community is key to its ongoing development and growth. Encourage good practice in all areas and you will reap the benefits.

The public

What will you have to do to enjoy 'the goodwill of all the people' (Acts 2.47)? A good reputation is a priceless asset. It witnesses to the Kingdom, opens doors and makes it easier to win backing for the venture.

If your fresh expression is to be 'a good citizen', you will need to think about:

- **legal requirements.**

    These include child protection, health and safety, employment law, third party insurance and charitable status.

- **other agencies and churches.**

    These range from the police, to the school, to local voluntary organisations, to churches in the neighbourhood. Who will need to be consulted or kept informed as the venture develops?

- **links with representatives.**

    These might include the local residents association or, in a workplace context, a union or employee representative.

- **ethical boundaries.**

    These could include conflicts of interest and transparency in how you operate.

Partners

Partnering with a secular organisation or local churches could well enable your missional community to extend its networks, leverage extra resources and increase its impact.

But wisdom is also needed to avoid partnerships that become a distraction (leading to a loss of focus), rather than furthering the venture's objectives.

Getting feedback

By paying close attention to prayer supporters, those you are serving, people who open doors, the public and partner organisations, you will increase trust in what your fresh expression is doing.

This will enable you to draw on a wide pool of wisdom and generate a goodwill that will help fuel the initiative in future.

expressions: making a difference
Fresh Expressions, 2011,
978-095600054-5
Chapter 27: Wolverhampton Pioneer Ministries

Wolverhampton Pioneer Ministries has developed a very good model of partnerships for their city-centre work.

how can we find our way?

Share booklet 05

This *Share booklet* is one of a series which aims to help you to think about how to start, support and sustain a fresh expression of church.

01 how can fresh expressions emerge?

02 how should we start?

03 what should we start?

04 how can we get support?

05 how can we find our way?

06 how can we be sustainable?

07 how can we be a great team?

08 how can we finance a fresh expression?

09 how can we encourage a fresh expression?

10 how should we teach and preach?

Contents

Planning ahead	71
A fresh expressions journey	72
What makes you who you are?	76
Milestone reviews	78
Mission Action Plans	80
Checking the compass	82

Planning ahead

How can we find our way? is about envisaging the journey ahead by making sense of the route already travelled.

Learning through experience

This booklet does not offer you a step-by-step model but will highlight the involvement of the missional community and teams, their prayerful learning through experience and how that learning is applied in the next stage of the journey.

You will need to consider what makes you who you are, how to assess and review your progress and how to continually check that you are following God's leading and guidance.

A fresh expressions journey

Looking forward entails imagining your fresh expression's journey. One way that many ventures are likely to emerge is outlined below.

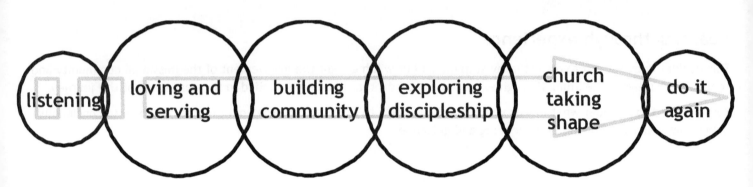

underpinned by prayer, ongoing listening and relationship with the wider church

Which way do we go?

This is a simplified description of what can be a messy process, and often the pathway will look different because of the context. It involves envisaging the next steps in your journey and asking how to travel well.

Looking to the future prayerfully is important to:

- **discern the Spirit.**

  'What pathway is the Holy Spirit laying down for us?' The kingdom comes to us from the future, like seeing through the mist the faint outline of a distant city. Out of the mist appears a runner calling with news about what the city is like, shouting out suggestions about which path to take and pointing to the help he has provided en route. Looking forward entails straining to catch the runner's words and to see where he is pointing.

- **look for the next horizon and maintain the mission focus.**

  Fresh expressions can easily plateau if they don't have a new challenge.

- **prepare adequately.**

  Practical questions may include such things as getting charitable status.

How do fresh expressions develop?
freshexpressions.org.uk/guide/develop

- **avoid pitfalls.**

  Some fresh expressions have suffered because Christians flooded into the new venture, changed the atmosphere unintentionally and reset the agenda. Looking forward can help you to avoid this and other problems.

- **build in sustainability.**

  Sustainability should be factored in from an early stage, not be something you think about later. What do you have to do now to help your fresh expression have a long life?

In the initial stages, the leadership team may ask questions like:

- how might people experience community as the venture develops?
- how will the developing missional community (or team) live out its relationship with Jesus?
- as church begins to take shape, what might discipleship (including worship) look like?
- is the fresh expression starting in ways that will be sustainable?
- what do we have to do next?

You won't be able to answer all these questions at the beginning. But they may help you to be intentional about the DNA you are implanting in the venture. Remember: how you begin is likely to determine the sort of fresh expression that emerges.

Later challenges may include:

- travelling to the next stage of the journey.
- transitioning from the current leader to the next.
- how do we start another fresh expression, so that this is not just a one off?
- adapting to changes in context.

Looking forward should be a continuous activity. It will help you to avoid becoming so preoccupied with 'keeping the show on the road' that you to settle into comfortable routines and things grow stale.

Looking back becomes important as the venture begins to develop. It focuses on how God has led you in recent months and over a longer period. This provides a perspective from which to look ahead.

It is a means for the Spirit to teach you through your experience. You might want to prayerfully use Sue Ballard and John Pritchard's 'pastoral cycle':

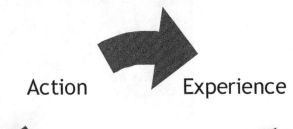

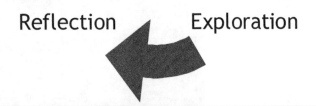

 expressions: making a difference
Fresh Expressions, 2011,
978-095600054-5
Chapter 21: The Lounge at Costa

The Lounge at Costa are constantly evaluating what is working and trying new things.

Experience
What have we experienced on our journey, and within the missional community? How does each of our perceptions of what we have experienced differ?

Exploration
So what's been going on? In particular, what factors have shaped our experience?

Reflection
How does God see this? What would make him thrilled? What would make him weep? What would Jesus do in the light of the journey so far?

Action
What do we need to do as a result of our exploration and reflection?

This cycle should be a continuous process. When you take action, you begin to change the situation. New dynamics come into play which you experience, explore, reflect on and act upon, and these again change the situation. Over time, you become changed.

 Practical Theology in Action
Paul Ballard and John Pritchard,
SPCK, 2006, 978-028105719-1, ch6

Church for the Night

Church for the Night meets at Bournemouth parish church in the heart of club land.

The aim is not to 'pounce' on any of the town's clubbers who may come in but instead offer a free café and art installation - using projections, smoke machines, light ambient dance music, and a chilled out atmosphere - to help them find space with God.

Church for the Night, held every two months in St Peter's Church from 11pm until the early hours, has featured a variety of themes, including The Friendship of God. This involved 'building' a front door and a room inside the church for people to ring the bell, go in, and answer such questions as, 'What would you say to God if he lived next door to you?'

The theme of God of the Universe was opened up through the installation of science dome housing a 360 degree cinema which mapped the stars. It also included a talk from a scientist about the cosmos. Up to 600 people came through the church that evening, mainly to sit at the front, write a prayer card, light a candle and make the most of the free cakes that Mothers' Union members had made for them.

Church for the Night is exploring what it is to be church within a different context and a different culture, looking at issues like discipleship and values - with humility, servanthood, and accountability through 'D' (discipleship) groups at its core.

The thinking also extends to how they view hospitality, giving, mission and serving one another - among other things - so that people get a real sense of what they are all about as a group and begin to build an identity without having an attitude of being 'in' or 'out'.

This experience, exploration and reflection is very much seen in Sue Ballard and John Pritchard's 'pastoral cycle'. They are now looking for the next step in the work of Church for the Night as a community which focuses on living life together, eating together, praying together, and getting involved in social action with Worship, Word, and Witness.

What makes you who you are

It is important to know the 'distinguishing marks' of your fresh expression. How does it differ from others of a similar vein and what are the values that undergird everything you do?

Values

Looking back will enable you to review the fresh expression's values. The fresh expression's values are distinctive values, specific to this particular expression of church. They are values that mark the venture out from the genre - just as the values of the Northumbrian community, for example, differ to those of the Franciscans and other intentional communities.

A fresh expression will also have 'mission values' - see Share ✢ *How should we start?* (*Share booklet 02*). These are core values that could be expressed in a variety of situations. They are determined by the missional community in the very early stages, and shape its shared life and how it goes about its task as a team.

> **BOOK**
> **How should we start?**
> (Share booklet 02)
> Michael Moynagh, Andy Freeman, Fresh Expressions, 2011, 978-095681232-2

Sometimes fresh expressions get initial team and distinctive values confused. At the start of their work they ask, 'What values should shape this venture?' They hope for values that will be specific to the new venture, but find these difficult to discern. The venture has hardly started, so the values particular to it remain unclear.

Necessarily, values at the outset have to be rather general. They tend to be values that could apply to any number of fresh expressions. Their purpose is to guide the missional community's life and actions, and should be developed with this in mind.

Only as the fresh expression takes shape, and perhaps church within it, will the values that reflect the life of this specific body of people become apparent. They emerge in retrospect, and can be identified as part of the 'looking back' activity. They can be seen as gifts from God. They are charisms that give the emerging fresh expression its special flavour - gifts that bless its members and people outside.

In time, a fresh expression will develop:

- **initial team values;**
  These steer the missional community in its task.
- **distinctive values;**
  These mark the fresh expression out from others, the particular gifts God has given it.
  Some of the initial team values might well morph into more distinctive values as the fresh expression grows.

- **objectives;**

    These are goals that the team prayerfully sets well before distinctive values emerge.

    One goal might be that people served by the venture have opportunities to encounter Christ.

- **methods;**

    These are the means used to achieve these objectives.

    To create opportunities to encounter Christ, for example, people served by the venture can post prayer requests on to a prayer board.

- **strategy.**

    This is the overall picture, the methods being used to start and grow the fresh expression.

An example of a community's distinctive values can be found in the Potters House, Stoke on Trent. Their values are to be Spirit-filled, prayerful, creative, friendly and welcoming, young at heart, inclusive and compassionate, having high standards, culturally relevant, relational and collaborative (thepottershouse.eu/index.php?P=Who-Are-We).

Special characteristics

Remember that these distinctive values are most naturally discerned by looking back on the community's journey and asking, 'What are the special characteristics that God has given to us - things that seem to be a blessing to others and to us?'

These values may emerge gradually and take time to recognise. Perhaps periodically, as part of looking back, your missional community could ask whether any distinctive values seem to be apparent, and prayerfully compile what might be a provisional list. It might for example ask the community as a whole, and perhaps one or two people outside, whether they can identify features that make this particular venture stand out.

Over a period, it might distil these suggestions, try the list out on people and see if a consensus emerges. The aim should not be to have a long or comprehensive list, but just a few items that seem to capture what is unique to the community. A good sign might be when people say, 'Yes! That's us. That's really important!'

In smaller fresh expressions - based say in a home or workplace - it might be more difficult to distinguish between initial team and distinctive values. The first is likely to have a significant influence on the second. The important thing is to recognize and own the values you have.

Milestone reviews

Reviews are intentional opportunities to take stock and envisage the road ahead. They also offer a good context in which to look back and look forward, involving the whole community or just the leadership team.

Time to take stock

Reviews can be done informally by two friends chatting over coffee or formally as an agenda item in a team meeting. The important thing is to do them regularly and take them seriously because they:

- **build discipline into your learning.**

    Looking forward and looking back involves learning from experience and applying this learning to the future. But this learning can be uncomfortable. It may involve giving up something you thought you knew or an established pattern of thinking.

- **help you adapt to changes in the context.**

    If you don't have reviews, members of the missional community may have no forum in which to express concerns or explore new opportunities. Issues may get buried and be addressed too late.

- **enable you to manage important transitions**

    For instance, the beginnings of church within the community, the arrival of a new leader or the decision to start another fresh expression as an offshoot. Milestone reviews are a good framework in which to begin the necessary conversations.

expressions: making a difference
Fresh Expressions, 2011,
978-095600054-5
Chapter 19: Streetwise

Streetwise began as a project meeting physical need, but after a review is now taking a more holistic approach.

Milestone reviews have something of a Eucharistic feel to them. They are a corporate activity, analogous to what happens at Holy Communion: the community looks back to what Jesus has done and looks forward to his return.

Milestone reviews could be undertaken within the context of an informal Communion or agape supper. This would combine worship, reflection and planning.

Dwight D. Eisenhower, the World War II general and later US President, once said:

> *Plans are worthless, but planning is everything.*
> **Dwight D. Eisenhower, Speech to the National Defense Executive Reserve Conference, 14/11/57**

The same is often true of fresh expressions.

The world is complex and fast changing, and missional communities leading fresh expressions are not in control of outside events. They have to watch out for opportunities, which may crop up unexpectedly, and seize them as they occur. In a world of flux, leadership by strategic plan should give way to leadership by discernment.

Missional communities should go with what presents rather than with what members thought was going to happen. 'Push when it moves' might be a good motto. Milestone reviews provide an opportunity to detect the Spirit's activity in a changing landscape.

Planning is indispensable because:

- **long-term planning is an opportunity for members of the missional community to have a conversation about their expectations.**

    At a later review, the community can prayerfully revise its expectations in the light of new knowledge, which then prompts further questions, 'What have we learnt? How do things look now?'

- **short-term planning is necessary for the team to know what to do next.**

    But seeing next steps from a planning-not-plans perspective allows team members to be reasonably relaxed if they have to adjust their actions in the light of circumstances. At the next milestone review, members can hold each other to account for making any changes.

Mission Action Plans

A Mission Action Plan (MAP) is one way to express the next steps, perhaps in the context of the team's longer term hopes. MAPs will vary according to the context. Larger ventures may develop quite sophisticated MAPs, while smaller ones may use something very simple. There is no one way to write a MAP.

Finding the best route

One possibility would be for your MAP to answer four questions:
- what are your plans for between now and when you next meet?
- how will you do it?
- who will do it?
- when will it be done by?

Another possibility would be to have four sections:
- a summary of your vision.
- a statement of the missional community's core values and any distinctive values that are starting to emerge.
- a short list of goals - what you hope to achieve by a specified date.
- a description of the tasks, by whom and when, to achieve these goals.

The task descriptions can form the basis of a simple statement of 'ministry expectations' for each team member (and any other volunteers), so that all are clear about what they are being asked to do and their boundaries.

Evaluation should be another part of the milestone review process. It is a way of discerning where and how the Spirit has been at work so that you can envisage how the Spirit might be leading you in future.

Measurement and target-setting has had a bad press, often because the targets are not owned by those involved. On the other hand, feedback from clients and staff is vital if you want to improve what you are doing.

A 'feedback' rather than 'target' approach to measurement can make a lot of sense within fresh expressions. Feedback can be a means of evaluating what the Holy Spirit has been doing.

Stuart P. Robinson and Mark Ireland have detailed discussion of MAPs.

Starting Mission-Shaped Churches
Stuart P. Robinson, Gospel Outreach Ministries, 2007, 978-095798321-2, ch8-13

How to do Mission Action Planning. A Vision Centred Approach
Mark Ireland, SPCK, 2009, 978-028106122-8

Moot

Story

The Moot monastic community offers hospitality and welcome in the City of London to 'questers' or 'spiritual seekers'. Moot members seek to deepen the ways they encounter God, themselves and others in community, spiritual formation and mission.

The community's worship draws deeply on the sacramental and contemplative traditions, aspiring to a common rhythm of life that expresses a commitment to living sustainably, holistically and justly.

In the city, Moot regularly meets people looking for resources to support their search for meaning, spiritual experience and practice. As a result Moot has been experimenting with two forms of welcome and hospitality - as part of their rhythm of life - for those resistant to traditional forms of church and evangelism.

One such welcome comes through Free Meditation sessions at Moot's 'home' in St Mary Aldermary Church, Watling Street. A group of 15 to 20 people meets every week to be led through a series of relaxation exercises into a silent meditation.

Another welcome, in a large pub in the area, sees a group meet for a 'Serum discussion' based on questions around life, God and spirituality. Starting with an icebreaker in which everyone introduces themselves, the session continues with a discussion starter and question to consider. The group then splits up into smaller groups and the ground rules of Serum are explained; the goal is not 'to win the argument' or 'get the right answer', the goal is mutual learning.

Moot has found that this approach works well, with the Christian presence and voice in the minority, because people find it much easier to listen when they no longer feel threatened by an atmosphere of dominance or control. It is not about asking people to move towards the church but instead providing a genuine space for dialogue.

Moot, through leadership by discernment, has looked out for opportunities to serve and made the most of them as they occur. They have focused on what presents itself rather than with what members thought was going to happen. Prayer continues for the discernment to recognise what may develop in future.

Checking the compass

It is all too easy to become caught up in the day-to-day workings of your fresh expression without assessing how it is going. How does it react to opportunities for growth or deal with challenges both inside and outside the church? The Spirit blows as it will - but have you set the sails to travel in His power?

How can we flow with what the Spirit is doing?

A first step would be to decide what you need to know. You might want to group your thinking around the four sets of relationships that are at the heart of church:

- **UP relationships toward God;**
- **OUT relationships in serving the world;**
- **IN relationships of fellowship within the gathering;**
- **OF relationship with the wider church (the gathering is part of the whole body).**

How well is your fresh expression growing in these four sets of relationships? To answer this you might need to identify appropriate indicators, such as the number of new people who have started to come regularly.

Charities often use quite sophisticated tools to evaluate softer outcomes - see, for example, homelessoutcomes.org.uk - and these might be adapted if you are a larger venture. Whatever you do, keep it as simple as possible.

A second step would be to decide how to collect the information. For example, you might have a discussion with a representative group from within the fresh expression, distribute a simple questionnaire or ask people outside the fresh expression (such as the head teacher in the school where you meet) about what impact they think it has had.

A third step would be to decide how you intend to use the results - for instance:

- **to inform the team's thinking, as part of milestone reviews?**
- **to aid reflection within the emerging community as a whole, perhaps through discussion during a gathering?**

These suggestions are intended to help you, and those within your missional community, to steer between no planning on the one hand and too much planning on the other. You will navigate the uncharted waters together.

how can we be sustainable?

Share booklet 06

This *Share booklet* is one of a series which aims to help you to think about how to start, support and sustain a fresh expression of church.

01 how can fresh expressions emerge?

02 how should we start?

03 what should we start?

04 how can we get support?

05 how can we find our way?

06 how can we be sustainable?

07 how can we be a great team?

08 how can we finance a fresh expression?

09 how can we encourage a fresh expression?

10 how should we teach and preach?

Contents

What is in your DNA?	87
What does sustainability involve?	88
Sustaining the pioneer	90
Shaped for the context	91
Handing over leadership	92
Dealing with problems	94
Keeping the venture fresh	97

What is in your DNA?

How can we be sustainable? is about considering sustainability in the very early stages of a fresh expression of church, not when the venture is well underway.

The long and the short of it

This booklet does not offer you a step-by-step model but will explore how, far from being an after-thought, sustainability needs to be in the fresh expression's DNA - or basic makeup.

Sustainability includes discipleship, worship and much else. This booklet focuses on some of the organisational aspects of keeping the emerging Christian community fruitful and fresh.

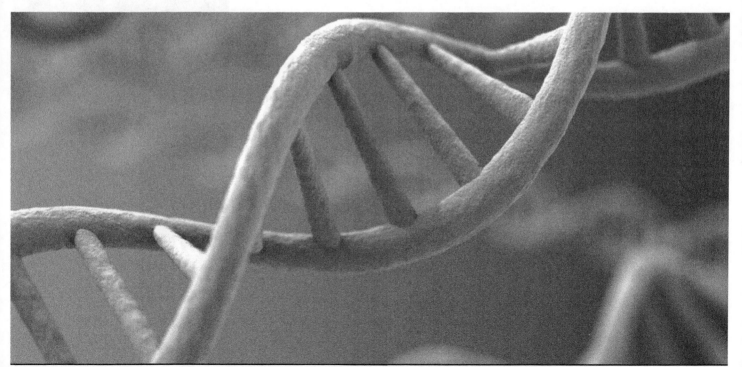

What does sustainability involve?

Are you trying to develop your fresh expression but don't know which way to turn? Take time to look at opportunities from a different angle. It can be all too easy to get stuck in a rut but a new way of thinking may lead to some radical results.

Choosing the right 'lens'

Sustainability in church planting has tended to be understood in terms of the 'three selfs', which were formulated separately by the 19th century missionary strategists, Henry Venn and Rufus Anderson. On this view, fresh expressions should become:

- **self-financing;**
- **self-governing;**
- **self-reproducing.**

There is also a fourth self that some have recently added:

- **self-theologising.**

A sustainable venture will develop a 'local theology' that responds to its context.

This 'three/four selfs' approach can hit problems if it is applied to fresh expressions through the lens of inherited church. You can end up assuming that a new church will be rather like existing churches, just as many 'daughter' churches were in the past.

The new church will become financially independent with its own minister, its own church council, its own representatives in the denominational structures and it may go on to plant a further church, which will take a similar form.

But if you apply the three/four selfs in a contextual way, you may end up thinking quite radically - more radically than has sometimes happened with fresh expressions.

A teenage congregation might interpret 'self-financing' as relying on two part-time youth workers, both of whom are financially self-supporting because they have part-time jobs.

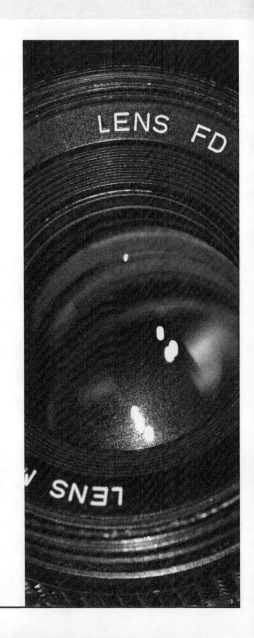

Bob Hopkins, *The 3-Self Principle - which end of the telescope?*, ACPI
tinyurl.com/acpi3self

Self-reproducing might involve new believers finding one or two other Christians in their work or their street, and starting a very small expression of church in the midst of their everyday lives.

Self-governing might be understood not as the fresh expression being independent of its parent church, but as having responsibility for its affairs within the governance structures of the local church.

Ultimately, if we are to use the three/four selfs criteria, we must think about financial sustainability, leadership and multiplication in ways that fit the context.

Despite their possibilities, the three/four selfs are still open to criticism. Do they downplay interdependence? Is the model too static for all fresh expressions?

So perhaps we should understand sustainability differently as a fresh expression. This would involve being:

- **connected to the wider church;**

    In relationships of mutual respect and support, so that the fresh expression helps to sustain the whole body and receives from it.

- **appropriately responsible;**

    The degree of financial, administrative and other responsibility will vary from one context to another and be appropriate to the context.

- **viable for its life span;**

    Some new churches will be seasonal, others longer term. The accent should be on viability while the community lasts rather than always assuming permanence.

- **attentive to flow.**

    Fresh expressions will manage the flow of their members to another Christian community, where appropriate, so that individuals have a sustained church involvement. If individuals need to change church as their spirituality evolves or circumstances change, they will be helped to do so. Sometimes sustainability will be more about flow than durability.

It will be important not to fill in these details too early to avoid prejudging what the fresh expression will be like. The meaning of 'appropriately responsible', for example, may only become apparent as the emerging church develops. We must not close down possibilities by prejudging how the Spirit will lead.

Sustaining the pioneer

Caring for the 'carers'. Spare more than a thought for the pioneer who is busy thinking of everyone else.

Whatever the size of venture, it is easy for leaders to get burnt out and put the church-start at risk. To a significant extent, the health of the Christian community will be bound up with the well-being of its leaders.

Selecting the right people is an obvious first step in sustaining pioneers, while attending to their walk with God will be pioneers' own first responsibility.

Appropriate support should be available - either arranged by the pioneer, or by the pioneering team or with the help of those to whom the pioneer is accountable.

Experience tells us that pioneers need:
- **someone to cry and laugh with;**
- **a spiritual director or companion;**
- **prayer support;**
- **appropriate training;**
- **a coach or mentor who can both listen and advise from experience;**
- **advice and support from others in a similar field;**
  Preferably from someone who has planted a fresh expression in a similar context or been involved in a comparable type of venture.
- **specialist expertise.**
  For example in finance, legal and other matters.

ENC

Changing from one size to another also leads to changes in how people connect with each other and those around them. In the early days of Exeter Network Church (ENC), everybody used to pitch in and do everything together - now it's too big to even know everyone.

Started in 2005, today's ENC is a church of about 350 people based on a collection of networks. Along the way, the challenge of sustainability has led them to radical re-thinks of how and where they operate.

ENC made history in 2009, being granted the Church of England's first Bishop's Mission Order and saying that it gave them a 'mandate to be missional' through connectedness with the wider church. But they have worked hard to avoid unhelpful duplication - rather than multiplication - in their networks. It's a challenge to keep the missional focus but the church's trajectory is to see what God is doing in Exeter and join in.

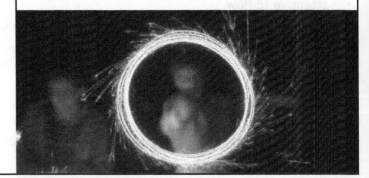

Shaped for the context

From the earliest days, founders of church should be asking, 'What sort of venture would be sustainable in this context?' Becoming sustainable begins with the intention to be sustainable.

How do you measure up?

This will raise issues of size and leadership. What size of venture is appropriate in this context? In particular, what size of venture is appropriate for the leadership gifts that are likely to be available?

It may be significant that the early church was based on the home. This meant that each household church was formed around an existing structure of leadership - the head of the family. Where in your context are the existing leaders, and what might church look like if it was built round them?

Being contextual is especially vital in relation to financial sustainability. Good questions to ask early on might include:

- what are the financial resources of the people we are called to serve?
- what sized initiative could they realistically sustain?
- for how long will the initial funding be available and is replacement funding from outside likely?
- what resources can the wider body of Christ realistically contribute, and for how long?

Handing over leadership

This is one of the most difficult decisions to contemplate. Who will be there when it is time for you to hand over the reins - and what is the best way for it to happen?

Who's next in line?

Working sustainably means thinking about transitioning from first to second generation leaders. A good mindset is to remember that the project is 'with' not 'for' the people the venture serves. So when will they be able to take ownership of it and run it?

When should you transition? About a century ago the missionary, Roland Allen, argued that missionaries should allow their converts to stand on their own feet as soon as possible.

He pointed out that St Paul rarely stayed with his new congregations for more than six months. Missionaries, he claimed, should move on rapidly in a similar way, relying not on their continued presence to sustain the new community, but on Scripture and the Holy Spirit.

expressions: making a difference
Fresh Expressions, 2011,
978-095600054-5
Chapter 13: re:generation

re:generation has a deliberate policy of identifying emerging leaders.

Missionary Methods - St Paul's or Ours?
Roland Allen, Martino Fine Books, 2011,
978-1614270379, ch8-10

There is an opposing view. Time and again, Paul left his new churches quickly because of local opposition rather than through choice (e.g. Acts 13.50; Acts 14.5-6, 20; Acts 17.5-10, Acts 13-14). Indeed, after being driven out of Thessalonica, Paul became highly anxious about the fate of his fledgling church there (1 Thessalonians 1.17-2.5). He seems to have worried that he had had to leave too soon.

In Corinth and Ephesus, where he had greater freedom, he stayed for over 18 months and three years respectively. Leaving new churches very quickly does not seem to have been Paul's intentional strategy.

Moving on rapidly may have been easier for Paul than it is sometimes for us. Paul's churches seem to have been built around converts from the local synagogue, where Paul typically started his missionary work (Acts 14.1).

These Jews and 'God-fearing Gentiles' knew their Scriptures - our Old Testament - well (Acts 17.11). So, appointing leaders from among them may not have been as much of a challenge as it is in some circumstances today, when new believers may have virtually no Biblical knowledge.

Jesus provides an alternative model. His departure at the ascension left the disciples humanly responsible for the formation and expansion of the church. He intentionally delegated his leadership.

Those assuming responsibility were far from being the finished article. Matthew tells us that some of the 11 disciples (it could read 'many') still doubted (Acts 28.17). Yet Jesus did not allow these doubts to derail his delegation. Rather, he embedded the principle of handing over leadership in the very origins of the church.

However, unlike Allen's account of St Paul, Jesus did not exit after only a few months. His closest disciples spent some three years with him, day after day. This was mentoring of a highly intense kind.

If the Jesus picture emphasises the importance of proper formation before passing on leadership, Paul's experience - despite often being driven by necessity - suggests that in some situations the hand-over can be remarkably fast.

The two pictures qualify each other. Paul's warns against raising the bar of Christian maturity too high before handing over leadership. Jesus warns against being too optimistic about the time it will take church founders to accomplish their task. The timing of when to move on requires discernment in context.

How might you discern? When they left, both Jesus and Paul left behind:

- **the Holy Spirit;**
- **a basic understanding of the gospel;**
- **the Old Testament - the equivalent of our Bible;**
- **Leadership;**
- **baptism and Holy Communion;**
- **in Paul's case, ongoing support - he kept in touch through his letters and his network of co-workers.**

Might whether these are in place be some helpful criteria for deciding when to leave?

Risk is always the big worry. Pioneers and others understandably fear that things may go wrong if the pioneer leaves too early. But that was same problem that Paul faced - and things did go wrong! Think of the church in Corinth!

Leadership involves learning by experience, including mistakes. Mistakes are the price of allowing new Christians to grow in their leadership gifts. It is a real price, but the gain is greater maturity and human flourishing.

Managing other transitions. Like most organisations, as a fresh expression starts and grows there will be times when it faces the challenge of making - for it - a significant transition.

One simple model suggests that the process of adaptive change involves three stages; 'initial organising' as a new venture develops, then 'mounting tension' as problems arise and finally a 'new emerging configuration' as solutions are found.

Dealing with problems

It is vital to know what to do when your fresh expression encounters inevitable stumbling blocks along the way. Going back to basics as to what you're doing and why will help to steer the venture back on course.

Challenge of change

When difficult problems arise, it helps to:

- **go back to your fundamental values;**

    'What are we about?' 'What are we trying to achieve?'

    This allows you to focus on the wood rather than the trees.

- **agree the principles that will guide how these values are expressed;**

    A cell-based church intending to grow further cells might agree four principles: each cell will have a mission focus, they will meet at least three times a month, their leaders will meet regularly in an accountability group and the cells will cluster together once a month.

- **allow maximum flexibility within these principles.**

    This freedom permits individuals to be creative within a framework that serves the venture's purpose, and this releases energy and generates fresh thinking.

Such an approach gives expression to Paul's vision in Romans 12 and 1 Corinthians 12 of shared ministry within the body, and reflects something of the way that Christ exercises servant leadership within the kingdom.

 expressions: making a difference
Fresh Expressions, 2011,
978-095600054-5
Chapter 23: The Sunday Sanctuary

The Sunday Sanctuary leaders are open to their fresh expression changing and evolving.

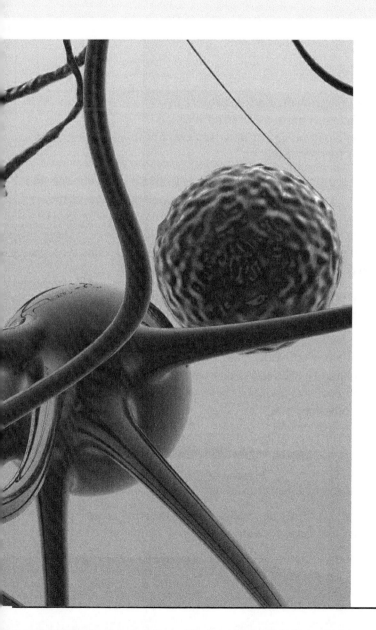

Some fresh expressions will need to become more strategic in their approach, as they get established and bear fruit. In the early days they could 'make it up as they went along' because they were discovering what would work in their setting. But having become established, they not only know what works for them, but they may also have become part of the local landscape, with links into the community and to other networks and churches.

Their experience, knowledge and connections with other people may mean that the situation feels not so totally out of their control. Depending on their size, they may be able to exert a certain amount of influence on their context. Instead of being at the mercy of events, to a small extent they may be in a position to shape local events.

All this may require different types of leadership and different forms of leadership structure. This is not really a shift from pioneering to pastoral leadership, which unhelpfully polarises the two. Pioneers need to pastor and pastors need to encourage innovation. The transition is more about an increased level of organisational complexity and the need for a greater emphasis on strategic thinking at the expense of ad hoc improvisation.

New skills may be required within the fresh expression to manage this transition and lead the church into the next phase of its life. Recognising that the venture has reached this stage is the first step to managing the transition effectively.

Grafted

Story

As a Church-Army-backed project in the Scottish borders, Grafted is based in the small village of Newcastleton but its work reaches much further afield.

They see their role as giving hope to those without hope and setting up and doing things that reflect the value of the church by 'being' rather than 'doing'. A drop-in centre at Hawick offers discipleship through its willingness to serve people and give genuine help to anyone who walks through the door.

Grafted works against the church's historic stance of demanding very high benchmarks of academic achievement for leadership, insisting that a lot of its work is as an onlooker to what the Holy Spirit is doing in growing the most unlikely of leaders.

The development of Refresh Community Church is one of the fruits of that work. About three quarters of the people who come are non-Christians with some 60 people from the community involved in one way or another. The aim of Refresh - comprising eight groups - is to encourage the development of missional people. As a result, church that's missional has become the norm' rather than an aspiration. It is something that has taken time to evolve.

At one point, a lot of people attending were Christians who wanted things to become more settled and comfortable. It was becoming a problem. The leadership went back to their fundamental values and responded by saying that, although Refresh worked well with traditional church in the area, they were called to be a mission group in the village. Their vision of Refresh was to be a lifeboat and resist the temptation to be a 'cruise liner'.

Some of those at Refresh are still involved with their local church and they did come close to meeting on a Sunday because of a desire to reach families but decided that wasn't the right way forward.

In the future, leaders hope that Refresh will continue to be guided by the very people that have come through their work at grass roots level.

Keeping the venture fresh

Running low on energy is a very real possibility after the adrenaline associated with establishing something new has gone. What can be done to ensure that your fresh expression has sufficient fuel to remain an effective force when initial excitement subsides?

Against the tide

There is a well-known process by which organisations become institutionalised. A leader with an inspirational vision forms a community, which stabilises in the second generation and formalises criteria for membership. In subsequent generations, much of the energy goes in maintaining and protecting established structures to ensure the community continues. Can fresh expressions avoid following this pattern?

Theologian John Drane identifies these temptations as a venture starts and grows:

- a concern for efficiency, such as replicating a model that has worked elsewhere - it seems quick and easy;
- a trend toward calculability, as demands grow to see numerical results;
- a desire for predictability - conformity to some pattern or other, perhaps inherited forms of worship;
- a desire to retain some form of control by existing churches.

He suggests four values that can work in the opposite direction:

- creativity as opposed to efficiency;
- relationality instead of calculability;
- flexibility (or adaptability) rather than predictability;
- proactivity - straining forward instead of holding on to the past - in place of control.

Resisting McDonaldization: fresh expressions of church for a new millennium
John Drane
in **Pioneers4Life: Explorations in theology and wisdom for pioneering leaders**
Dave Male (ed.), BRF, 2011, 978-184101827-0

So how can these four counter-values become the heartbeat of a fresh expression? Milestone reviews, suggested in Share➔ *How can we find our way? (Share booklet 05)*, offer one way.

Continuous review, which is central to the milestones approach, allows flexibility by making it easy to change course as necessary, flexibility will encourage creativity, involving people in the review process will promote relationality, while the looking forward aspect will foster proactivity.

How can we find our way
(Share booklet 05)
Michael Moynagh, Andy Freeman, Fresh Expressions, 2011, 978-095681235-3

Identifying fruitfulness is an important aspect of sustainability. It is a means of discerning where and how the Spirit is at work. It allows the question to be asked, as should be asked of an inherited church, whether a fresh expression is a fruitful or barren branch of the vine (John 15.1ff).

You might ask: In what ways are members of the venture growing in:

- **their relationships with God?**
- **serving people outside the venture?**
- **deeper fellowship?**
- **commitment to the wider body of Christ?**

Fruitfulness will be at the heart of a sustainable fresh expression, whether the venture is long-lasting or not. That is why we can prayerfully hope that as the Spirit works among us, fruit will be produced that endures and can be shared with others.

Sorted

Story

Keeping the venture fresh is at the heart of Sorted's work in Bradford. Church Army evangelist, and keen skateboader, Andy Milne started it in 2004 after getting to know the area's young skaters, many of whom went on to become founder members of the youth church.

Relationships were initially built through skateboarding but it's quite a small part of the Sorted 'package' now. They meet three times a week, seeing an average of 100 young people during that time. A Monday youth congregation, attracting 13 to 20-year-olds, gets involved in everything from setting up equipment to worship, teaching and prayer.

Tuesday nights are more discipleship-focused with five groups each led by two young people. Andy encourages them, saying that when they get involved in leadership it really helps their understanding. As they run it themselves, they 'own' it and the energy triples. Fridays see them have a testimony, short talk and different activities. The young people usually come through their friends or schools to these sessions because the Friday slot is very open and accessible. They get to know people and when there is a bit more trust they tend to move into the other two groups.

Some local churches realised they hadn't got the resources to do anything similar themselves but felt they could practically support something that's Kingdom work by allowing Sorted to use their buildings.

Sorted 2 was launched because organisers realised that about 80% of those in Sorted 1 were from the same 1200-pupil school. It is now running in the area's second school, the sixth largest secondary in the country with 1800 students.

A Church Army team now oversees the entire project. People from local churches also act as adult volunteers for each Sorted, this makes a tremendous difference because the schools' work is growing all the time.

This flexibility and proactivity in approach has also seen Sorted be granted a Bishop's Mission Order because it was noted at diocesan level that Sorted is not a seedbed for something else or an extension to another church. It's a church in its own right.

how can we be a great team?

Share booklet 07

This *Share booklet* is one of a series which aims to help you to think about how to start, support and sustain a fresh expression of church.

01 how can fresh expressions emerge?

02 how should we start?

03 what should we start?

04 how can we get support?

05 how can we find our way?

06 how can we be sustainable?

07 how can we be a great team?

08 how can we finance a fresh expression?

09 how can we encourage a fresh expression?

10 how should we teach and preach?

Contents

Hitting the right note	103
Forming	104
Norming	106
Storming	108
Performing	112
Adjourning	114

Hitting the right note

How can we be a great team? is about the vital importance of nurturing the team (or missional community) throughout a fresh expression's life.

Shaping the future

This booklet does not offer you a step-by-step model but explores how the missional community - whether large or small - enables the new church to emerge and sets its tone.

Research shows that in the business world teams of entrepreneurs rather than any one person found a substantial proportion, perhaps the majority, of new ventures.

A framework

Here is a well-established framework to explore some of the issues involved but puts the topics in a slightly different order than normal:

- forming;
- norming;
- storming;
- performing;
- adjourning.

These are not so much distinct stages as overlapping and often parallel aspects of a missional community's life. Each aspect is likely to be present in one way or other throughout the group's existence.

Forming

Forming the missional community will occur throughout the community's life as members join and leave. Forming involves members getting to know each other and establishing ground rules. It is about forming the community's identity. When you start hearing 'we' rather than 'I', you will know this process is well underway.

Getting to know you

Forming includes welcoming new members. Willing helpers may not be readily at hand, so realistic expectations are necessary. Keep the following in mind:

- **additions to the group have down as well as upsides.**

    Unless they are replacing someone, a new member will make the missional community larger and perhaps more complex. Leading it could become more demanding.

- **a more diverse group can improve the community's capacity.**

    The team will have a wider range of skills and networks. More diverse views can produce better decisions. But diversity may also reduce cohesion, increase conflict and cause an actual decline in effectiveness. The 'exchange theory' of groups maintains that individuals want to get out of a group at least as much as they put in. Balancing these considerations needs prayerful thought.

- **size may affect the time it takes the community to form.**

Forming should be about forming community, even if there are just two of you. If the missional community sets the tone for the fresh expression and community is essential to being church, then community must be at the heart of the team's life.

Teams with a community feel have an emphasis on horizontal relationships. Individuals don't just relate to the leader, they have strong ties to others in the team. There is a sense of shared decision-making and mutual support. Taking deliberate steps to get to know one another will start to create community. These might include doing things together, such as giving a meal together or going away for a day.

Warm-up exercises can encourage the sharing of experiences or stories. Doing a Myers-Briggs or Belbin Team Roles exercise will reveal members' gifts and deepen the team's sense of community.

> **The Complete Book of Questions: 1001 Conversation Starters for any Occasion**
> Garry Poole, Zondervan, 2003,
> 978-031024420-2

Encouraging individuals to share their lives is vital. Jesus and the disciples had close fellowship, as did members of the early church. The leader will play a key role by modelling openness: Jesus did not hide that he struggled in the Garden of Gethsemane - that's how we know! When leaders show they are incomplete, they open the door for others to help.

Reconnect

Story

Welcoming new members to help form missional community has been part and parcel of Reconnect's life since it came into being in Poole. As a newly-licensed pioneer minister in September 2008, Paul Bradbury set the ball rolling by renting an office in a café and then being quite disciplined about not 'doing' anything. For six months he and his wife Emily prayed, prayer walked, listened to what local residents were saying, chatted to those who knew the area and got a sense of what God was doing.

People were soon drawn to become part of the community because of its focus on making real friends with people - not just to tell them about the Gospel and the love of God but actually to get to know them and really to try and meet their needs in all kinds of physical ways as well as spiritual.

They found that forming community takes time. Other voices tried to tempt them to run an off the shelf programmatic approach to evangelism or mission but the recognition that relationship has to be built - and roots established - meant that it could not be rushed.

'Use the gifts that you've got' was a message that came through very strongly to them. This was demonstrated when a common interest in felt making brought together two people in a small group of 10 to start running felt making workshops. These sessions in turn developed into a monthly felt making group.

When later commissioned as a community, Reconnect members signed a rule of life – developed by looking at Acts and the gospels to find out what it means to be a community of disciples. As time went on, other initiatives began to emerge and Reconnect is now part of the Poole Missional Communities charity – set up to oversee and support the town's pioneering Christian work and protect the growing community's identity.

Reconnect's vision is to multiply the numbers of people who are opening their homes, engaging with those around them, using their gifts and talents - and working together to ensure a community that has Jesus at its core.

Norming

Norming (establishing shared values) occurs as members work together, developing close relationships of trust. It involves negotiating roles, relationships and task procedures. As such, it overlaps with 'forming'.

Share and share alike

This phase is complete when members accept a common set of expectations about how to do things. But the process may restart when a significant new member joins or a significant transition occurs in the fresh expression's life.

Spiritual norms should be nurtured as a priority. They will centre on members' inner hearts. Addressing the inner heart includes clearing it of barriers to healthy relationships.

This clearing process, which is ongoing, is a work of the Spirit. The Spirit of Christ, who self-emptied himself to the extreme of death, cleanses the inner heart of its preoccupation with self. Prayer and other spiritual practices are used by the Spirit to do this. Clearing a path for the Spirit within the team is ultimately the leader's responsibility, but might the team appoint a 'spiritual guide' for this purpose?

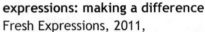

expressions: making a difference
Fresh Expressions, 2011,
978-095600054-5
Chapter 26: Tubestation

The original pioneers at Tubestation felt the need to appoint a spiritual director as the community developed.

Encouraging 'communal' norms is also essential and involves going the extra mile for others in the team. Members care for each other, which enhances team working by:

- **developing trust;**

    Individuals will be more likely to express emotions and accept the emotional expressions of others. This fosters open communications, which expands members' knowledge of others' motivations, goals and viewpoints and lessens misunderstandings that can undermine trust.

- **increasing identification;**

    Individuals understand each other better and so begin to see others' perspectives, resources and identities as extensions of their own.

- **strengthening the sense of mutual obligation**

    'One good turn deserves another'. Empathising with others increases the willingness to help. The team works better.

It is important, therefore, that the group keeps working at these 'communal' practices and does not take them for granted. Getting to know one another and sharing each others' lives should be part of norming, as well as forming.

Encouraging 'task' norms involves developing very simple understandings of how members will work together - from how often the team meets to what will happen during the meetings, such as the use of milestone reviews. See *How can we find our way? (Share booklet 05)*.

> **How can we find our way** BOOK
> (Share booklet 05)
> Michael Moynagh, Andy Freeman, Fresh Expressions, 2011, 978-095681235-3

How task-focused norms (which emerge as the work proceeds) become accepted helps to shape the community's life. For instance:

- **are norms set by the leader or agreed by the group as a whole?**

  The more that norms are owned by the group, the greater will be members' commitment to it.

- **how effectively are norms 'defended' by community members?**

  Norms that are upheld bring a degree of certainty and predictability to the group, which alleviates anxiety - especially helpful in pioneering contexts of uncertainty.

- **are norms intentionally reviewed from time to time?**

  For example, by periodically inviting members to comment on their ways of working and suggest improvements? Bringing to light difficulties will increase members' ownership of working arrangements.

Without 'the second mile' of communal norms, task-centred relationships can become mechanical, over-formal and rigid, with a loss of creativity. But a communal emphasis without appropriate task norms can produce an ill-disciplined team that fails to achieve its goals.

Communal and task norms, undergirded by self-emptying hearts, will build trust, group identity and mutual obligation. When team members face uncertainty and disappointment, their norms of working together will see them through.

Storming

Storming is usually put after forming, because there can be an uncomfortable period of jostling between members before the group settles down. But we list it third, at the centre of the five aspects of a missional community's life, to symbolise the central part that storming (or conflict) can be expected to play.

Agree to disagree

It helps to have realistic expectations. Conflict is natural in a healthy team. Think of all the disagreements among the disciples and in the early church!

Conflict:

- **may reflect the pioneering nature of the task.**

    Because the group is engaged in something new, it cannot always rely on previous knowledge. The resulting uncertainty and confusion may produce conflict, heightened by anxiety.

- **may reflect a healthy diversity within the group.**

    Different viewpoints allow issues to be considered from a variety of angles. Something important is less likely to be overlooked.

- **can be a sign that individuals are being given space - that no one is being suppressed.**

    Healthy communities may even encourage dissent to enable their members to flourish. Conflict can indicate that power in the group is dispersed.

- **can help to build community.**

    As team members share their real thoughts and feelings, endure the hurt of disagreement and find that they still accept each other at the end. Conflicts are the growing pains of community.

- **can provide good learning if handled constructively.**

    A new church that copes well with conflict will show how to use conflict fruitfully in other situations, which will be a blessing to society.

For these reasons, conflict should be welcomed when handled well. This positive attitude will reduce anxiety and give members greater confidence to face their disagreements. Agreed practices for handling disagreements may be helpful, negotiated as part of the norming process.

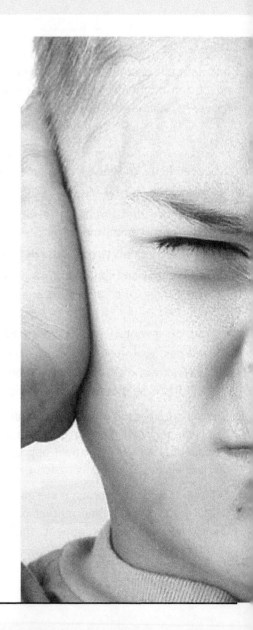

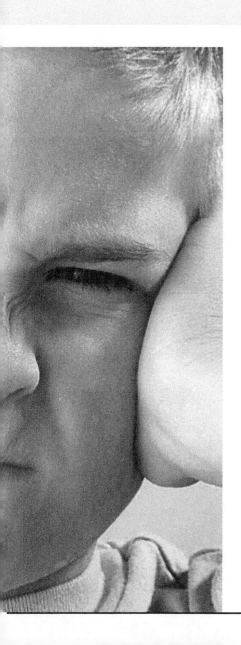

One youth church spent two evenings talking about how best to handle conflict. The teenagers came up with a host of ideas. These were distilled into some key principles, such as sort things out immediately and don't talk about others behind their backs.

A key leadership role is to articulate differences. When group members disagree, it is important that the leader keeps re-expressing the various views. The leader should do this whether or not they are chairing the meeting, and especially if they are a protagonist in the debate. Articulating the different views:

- **shows the parties that they have been understood, reducing anxiety.**

    Demonstrating that individuals have been heard is one of the few tasks the leader cannot delegate.

- **helps the parties understand each other.**

    Hearing the same point in different words can bring clarity, while hearing it expressed calmly can encourage a rational instead of an emotional response. The leader may comment that a view is strongly held, but conveying that information in an emotionally detached way will encourage greater detachment by others. Individuals are encouraged to process the group's feelings without being swamped by them.

- **allows contributions to be reframed so as to bring people together.**

    Comments can be re-expressed in a way others may understand. Especially when disagreements disrupt the group, might an outside facilitator help?

A time of quiet can give space for individuals to reconnect with the Spirit, distance themselves a little from the issues and get a wider perspective. They can be encouraged to pay attention to their inner hearts. What are they feeling strongly about? Why? Are there motives that should be taken to the cross?

Conflict is best managed within communities of grace. In 'grace-full' missional communities, members recognise their own flaws, weaknesses and need of forgiveness, making them more ready to forgive others. Forgiveness smothers resentment and enables conflict to be handled constructively.

How conflict is managed will do much to shape a team. If members learn to handle conflict constructively:

- **the missional community will feel safe;**
- **levels of honesty will rise;**

  This will strengthen community and aid performance.

- **a more diverse membership will be possible;**

  This will broaden the gifts, insights and network connections available to the community.

- **power is likely to be distributed more widely within the group.**

expressions: making a difference
Fresh Expressions, 2011,
978-095600054-5
Chapter 24: The Wesley Playhouse

At The Wesley Playhouse, converting a building for missional use was controversial but is now fully supported by the original congregation.

As the missional community evolves, with members joining and leaving, the leader would be wise occasionally to review their leadership style. If this can done openly with the team, what a sign of maturity!

Tubestation

Story

In 2006, a Methodist chapel overlooking a beach in north Cornwall decided to redesign its premises in a bid to make it more accessible to the surfers who flocked to the area all year round. Tubestation was the result.

The chapel building, transformed into a surf lounge internet café, also boasts facilities such as indoor skate ramps. It attracts high expectations from visitors but its leaders say everything hinges on the concept of love your neighbour.

As that concept has taken root in Polzeath, discipleship - both in small groups and with individuals - is on the increase. Trust is also being built up among the surfing community, so much so that Tubestation leaders were invited to lead a 'paddle out' for a professional surfer's funeral in which over 100 surfers paddled out to sea on their surfboards while the ashes were scattered in the water.

However not everything has gone smoothly as the work has developed. Tensions between existing church structures and Tubestation mean that dealing with conflict has been part and parcel of the fresh expression's growth. While being extremely grateful for the generosity of the Methodist Church in allowing Tubestation to come into being at all, leaders have grappled with the challenge of allowing new life to emerge without it being 'squashed' by more traditional ways of church working. The pioneering nature of the task is reflected in these challenges but the Tubestation community cite trust and generosity of spirit as being crucial - on both sides - if the challenges are to be successfully met and conflict resolved.

Tubestation was born out of the local Methodist circuit which gave leaders a blank canvas - and freedom - to make the initiative work. The temptation was to set up a church which was totally relevant culturally to surfers, diverging from the local, rather systematic, very traditional way of doing things. However Tubestation's decision to stay in a local circuit means that three years down the line, the community has a very diverse way of expressing its faith. Leaders see it as a very healthy thing, saying it is a united expression rather than an expression which has gone out on a tangent from local traditions.

Performing

Performing is the aspect of the missional community's life that concentrates on agreeing and then working toward shared goals.

What can we learn?

Performing centres on the continuous looking forward, looking back, milestone review, planning-not-plans and evaluation processes described in Share+ *How can we find our way? (Share booklet 05)*. Individuals will perform tasks generated by these processes.

How can we find our way (Share booklet 05) Michael Moynagh, Andy Freeman, Fresh Expressions, 2011, 978-095681235-3

Whether in a tiny or large group, members will require ongoing training and support. Many fresh expressions suffer because missional communities have not taken time to learn from other people.

Learning is at the centre of discipleship. It requires a humble spirit. How much time is your team spending in explicit learning? What does this say about your disposition of heart?

A missional community should consider its initial training needs:

- **learning the principles of birthing and growing a fresh expression;**

  Should members of the team attend a Fresh Expressions *vision day*, short course (*mission shaped intro*) or the one year part-time course (*mission shaped ministry*)?

- **personal evangelism;**

  You might seek advice from the Church Army, for example;

- **where appropriate, health and safety, child protection and the basics of financial management.**

The missional community will need ongoing support:

- **might someone in the community join a learning network and bring insights back to the group?**

  Learning networks enable practitioners to share experiences and wisdom, so as to avoid re-inventing the wheel.

- **might the community benefit from a coach or mentor?**

    Coaching need not always be one-to-one, it can involve whole teams. On-the-job coaching can be a highly effective form of training, though sadly it is not always available.

- **what reading might team members undertake?**
- **how will the community be spiritually nurtured?**
- **how will it remain connected to the wider church?**
- **what prayer support will the community receive?**

The team leader may need support over and above that available to the missional community, such as:

- **a spiritual director or guide;**
- **someone outside the community to cry and laugh with;**
- **practical support (where appropriate);**

    For instance moving house, getting started and finding specialist help;

- **accountability arrangements alongside practical support;**
- **further training in the principles and practice of fresh expressions, or in Biblical studies and theology.**

The leader's and team's spiritual health need particular attention. Some pioneers have been burnt out through the pressure of bringing a fresh expression to birth and team members can be left exhausted. So prioritising the emotional and spiritual well-being of leaders and teams should be a must, however small the new church.

Pioneering teams owe this to themselves, their families and friends, the venture they are leading and above all to God. If a church-start is to be truly the Spirit's work, time spent receiving from the Spirit must be a good investment.

Adjourning

Adjourning happens if the missional community disbands after a time. Maybe the attempt to start a fresh expression was not successful. Or perhaps the community was fruitful, but for a limited period.

Facing the truth

In such cases, endings must take place with dignity. If the missional community can let go, grieve, give thanks for what was, learn and share any lessons, and move on it will enable others in the fresh expression to do the same.

Team members will be helped to let go if they can share their reflections on their journey together and how they feel about the approaching end. Being honest about disappointments and jointly owning the responsibility (not blame) for any short-comings will help to ease the pain.

Mistakes can become a gift to the Kingdom if they can be a source of learning for the wider church. 'These are things that we would have done differently' can be hugely helpful to practitioners who are starting out.

 Share your stories
freshexpressions.org.uk/stories

When individuals leave the team, remaining members may learn much by asking their departing colleague what they most enjoyed in belonging to the group, have learnt from the experience and what issues the team might give further thought to.

Endings don't have to be loose ends. They can enrich the team and the wider church. In so doing, adjourning - alongside forming, norming, storming and performing - can nurture the leadership potential of the missional community.

expressions: making a difference
Fresh Expressions, 2011,
978-095600054-5
Chapter 25: 3:08 @ Kingshill

3:08 @ Kingshill in Nailsea came to an end after just two year, but the journey equipped its team for new things.

3:08 @ Kingshill

Story

When a group of people at Christ Church, Nailsea, realised that they weren't reaching families in one of its key areas, they decided to have a go at planting an all-age congregation in Kingshill CofE Primary School. It was easy to reach and attended by the children of many of the families they hoped to reach in that part of north Somerset.

Organisers did some research and opted for a monthly act of worship on a Sunday afternoon after discovering that non-churchgoers described the timings of many church events as 'not particularly helpful'. To avoid Sunday lie-ins, local football and shopping trips, they picked the 'memorable' time of 3:08pm - so 3:08 was born. A small core team leafleted every house in the neighbourhood, advertised in the school notice sheet and local newspaper, and spoke to everyone they met. But despite their efforts, the team never reached the people they really wanted to reach.

On launch day, 43 people turned up, many coming from local churches, but disappointingly there were few genuine newcomers. With hindsight the team felt they did too much 'getting on with it' and not enough thinking and talking about what people really wanted. They learned that if people tell you that a time of worship is not convenient, it does not then automatically mean that that those people would like to go at a different time. 3:08 leaders felt they may jumped to that conclusion a little too quickly.

For one or two people, 3:08 at Kingshill became their spiritual home but the majority of those attending were already churchgoers. After reviewing the progress of 3:08 in its second year, the team unanimously agreed that it should stop but they also felt happy at what had been achieved, enjoyed a celebratory last act of worship at 3:08 - and later discussed how the gifts and skills they had developed might be used in other ways. Many of those skills have now been ploughed back into Christ Church.

Although 3:08 didn't take off there are now two or three developing fresh expressions in the area which are currently working well. Nailsea sees it as a period of constant experiment.

how can we finance a fresh expression?

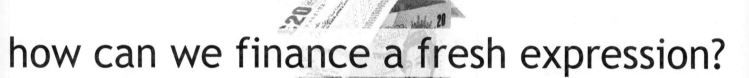

Share booklet 08

This *Share booklet* is one of a series which aims to help you to think about how to start, support and sustain a fresh expression of church.

01 how can fresh expressions emerge?

02 how should we start?

03 what should we start?

04 how can we get support?

05 how can we find our way?

06 how can we be sustainable?

07 how can we be a great team?

08 **how can we finance a fresh expression?**

09 how can we encourage a fresh expression?

10 how should we teach and preach?

Contents

Finance: planning and prayer	119
Attitudes to money	120
A project finance tool	122
Seven top tips	124
Sustainable finance	126
Resources	128
Appendix: Methodist funding	131

Finance: planning and prayer

How can we finance a fresh expression is about how to put down strong financial roots to allow for both start-up costs and long-term sustainability, helping you to weather the storms of economic instability.

Money, money, money

This booklet does not offer you a step-by-step model but explains how finance can be a critical factor in enabling the success or failure of fresh expressions, explores how our attitudes to money and finance are an important element in project planning and emphasises that both good theology and good financial planning are essential.

The booklet:

- explores attitudes to money and finance;
- gives a simple project planning tool to help with vision exploration;
- Outlines 'seven top tips' for the project planning and vision exploration;
- identifies the importance of sustainable income, including regular giving;
- gives some key resources in this area.

Attitudes to money

How we feel about money varies over time. It can be both good and bad! But money is an important element to manage as it can have a significant impact on shaping the development of vision and it is as much a theological as an economic issue.

A wide range

The amount of money needed to start a fresh expression will vary according to the type, size and scope of the initiative. A workplace fresh expression comprised of cell groups that meet at lunchtime may cost very little (eg. work:space in Poole). A community-based project in a converted pub with a full-time worker, or something like the LegacyXS skatepark and youth centre in Benfleet, will cost a lot!

What's the difference?

Developing sustainable income starts by understanding the distinction between 'capital' or 'start-up' income and ongoing income or 'revenue'.

The first type of income covers start-up costs: one-off costs such as the purchase of equipment. The second meets ongoing costs: regular expenses such as rent, putting money aside for salaries and to replace equipment. You need to estimate these costs at the outset. Of course, these estimates will change as plans get modified and the venture develops.

It can take several years to develop new income streams to cover ongoing costs. Meanwhile, grant-makers and others who contribute to start-up funding will want to restrict the time frame of their investment.

You need to be thinking well in advance about how your initiative will become self-supporting. It may be wise to project your expected annual costs and income (start-up and ongoing) over the medium to long term - three to five years if you are a large-ish venture. Again depending on size, the same should be done on a month-by-month basis over the next year or two.

For both sets of figures, are there any times when your costs will exceed your income? How will you make sure there will be enough cash in the bank to pay the bills?

"It's a necessary evil"

"It's scarce"

"It's spent on the wrong things"

"It's an enabler of mission"

Investment (noun)
To lay out money or capital in an enterprise with the expectation of profit

"It's a means to an end"

"It's a blessing from God"

"I feel guilty about having it"

More on these stories:

work:space
freshexpressions.org.uk/stories/workspace

Legacy XS
freshexpressions.org.uk/stories/legacyxs

 expressions: the dvd - 1: stories of church for a changing culture
Church House Publishing, 2006,
978-071514095-6   Chapter 2: Legacy XS

Legacy XS funded a purpose-built youth centre from a mix of trusts, gifts and fundraising.

freshexpressions.org.uk/resources/dvd1/02

Legacy XS: community youth centre/skatepark

The vision was to expand on the success of the existing Legacy Youth Congregation through a new purpose built youth centre in Benfleet. Legacy XS opened in March 2005.

The aims of the project are to meet the physical, emotional and spiritual needs of the young people of the community - directly through services and facilities at the Centre, or by acting as a network enabler between agencies such as schools, social services, police and the local authority.

Focused on a specific group, in this case primarily young people in or on the edge of the skater/BMX community, the centre incorporates a drop-in café and skatepark, open every day. It is also the base for the Legacy Youth Congregation.

Timeline

- June 2003: Legacy XS set up as a registered charity to raise funds and build an Indoor Skate Park and Youth Centre as an outreach into the community by St George's Church, New Thundersley. Support also came from St Mary's Benfleet, in whose parish the park is based.
- February 2004: Legacy Trust of Benfleet registered as a charity to raise funds and support staff and volunteers for Christian outreach in the centre and community.
- September 2004: subsidiary trading company created to manage the centre. The land on which the centre was built is on the edge of a public park and is held on a 21 year lease from the Local Authority with zero rent and rates.

The capital cost of setting up the Centre was approximately £550,000. Funding was obtained from charitable trusts, fundraising and regular giving from supporters from within St George's Church; some Government grants were obtained through the Crime & Disorder Reduction Partnership. The balance was funded by loans from two Legacy XS trustees. Loan repayment is a management priority over the creation of reserves for the long-term refurbishment of the Centre.

Annual costs are £83,000. Ongoing income includes a membership fee (from over 900 members), payment for use of the Skate Park, continued gift-aided donations from 15 church members and income from fundraising events.

Kick-starting the vision

How do you start to think about what it will cost to turn the vision of a fresh expression of church into a reality? And how do you inspire others to do the same? Here's a way of getting those sometimes difficult discussions off the ground.

Help! Where do I begin?

This section introduces a one-page project finance tool designed to help you with the early stages of assessing an idea; and trying to scope it in terms of cost.

To start off with, we will take a look at the different components of the tool. Ask your group or team to think of a possible project - they may have some idea in mind; they may have little or no idea. Pick a reasonable idea and run through the five questions.

Firstly, the project is summarised in one sentence (useful to make sure you are clear what the project is!) and major steps/elements identified.

Having identified a number of elements, the key costs are identified and allocated to one of three types of cost. These can then be totalled to have a rough estimate of the likely financial costs of the project being considered. (A similar exercise for volunteer staff may also be useful.)

The next stage is to focus on who might benefit - this is important both in determining that there are beneficiaries from the project and in identifying who might contribute. New Christians coming to faith may be one benefit, but try to draw out some others.

The final stage is to identify individuals or groups who might be willing to contribute to the costs of funding the project, and to determine which types of cost they might fund.

Once completed this finance tool gives a useful overview of the prospective project - its activities, costs, benefits and potential sponsors. This is largely a tool for scoping vision, rather than a detailed planner; and many projects will need more detailed budgeting as the project plans take shape.

 The Complete Guide to Creating and Managing New Projects for Voluntary Organisations Book
Alan Lawrie, Directory of Social Change, 2010, 978-190629440-3

Project finance tool

This tool helps you quickly scope a project and the likely financing requirement

1. In one sentence, describe what your project will achieve if successful.

2. What are the major activities or actions you need to launch your project?

3. List up to three major costs you will incur in each of these areas:

Start up or capital costs	Regular weekly or monthly running costs	Other costs that will occur periodically
Total:	Total:	Total:

4. Who will benefit from your project and what will the benefits be?

           benefits by

           benefits by

           benefits by

5. Who might be willing to contribute to the costs of the project?

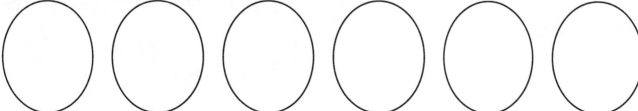

   Which type of costs might they each fund: start up, regular or periodic?

Seven top tips for money management

Have you ever despaired that finance seems to be a barrier rather than a lynchpin when forming a vision of what might be right in your own context? Despair no more. Here are seven tips on how to make money work 'for' you.

1. Separate costs

Separate out start-up costs from regular and periodic costs - they need to be funded differently.

2. Vision unlocks money

Vision unlocks money if it is compelling and clearly communicated.

3. Significant funding from individuals

A significant part of your funding is likely to come from individuals who find your vision compelling. This can be additional to current money coming into the church.

4. Individual funding can trigger grants

Additional grant funding can be triggered by funding from individuals.

The UK Church Fundraisers Manual: A Practical Manual and Directory of Sources
Maggie Durran, Canterbury Press Norwich, 2010, 978-184825002-4

5. Sustainable projects deliver benefits

A successful and sustainable project will deliver benefits to groups of people (physical or otherwise!)

6. Employment and property are key

Employing people and having buildings (purchase or rent) are major costs which impact a project's viability. These must be a particular focus for consideration and prayer.

7. Regular costs must be met by regular income

In time, regular costs will need to be met by regular income if the project is going to be sustainable.

Sustainable finance

We need to plan for success, and to think about where ongoing funding will come from. In many cases, if the fresh expression is successful it will build new worshipping communities who will learn to give as an integral part of their newly-discovered discipleship.

> expressions: the dvd - 1: stories of church for a changing culture
> Church House Publishing, 2006,
> 978-071514095-6
> Chapter 3: Taste and See
>
> Taste and See is a Café Church which runs the Café part as a viable business.

Growing finance with your initiative

Grants are a great help in the early years but much grant funding is only available for start up and capital costs.

Growing new Christians should develop discipleship that embraces stewardship and a desire to give to further the mission. Responsible Christian giving by those who are part of a fresh expression is key to sustainability.

A Church plant in the West Midlands town of Kingswinford was self-sustaining within two years. A core community of 30 people supported a full time pastor through their giving.

Some fresh expressions will have ongoing trading or service income to support the ongoing costs. For Taste and See in Kidsgrove, a café church, generates £600 a week through the café.

As the fresh expression grows, it may wish to express generosity more widely, encouraging mission in other places through gifts of money and expertise.

> **What does the Bible say about Stewardship?**
>
> *Now he who supplies seed to the sower and bread for food will also supply and increase your store of seed and will enlarge the harvest of your righteousness.*
> **2 Corinthians 9.10**

Registering as a charity
freshexpressions.org.uk/guide/starting/navigate/charity

The Charity Commission - Start up a charity
charity-commission.gov.uk/Start_up_a_charity

Charitable status

Setting up a charity can bring financial benefits, including Gift Aid, discounted help or advice and access to additional grant funding. However, establishing a charity does carry additional restrictions and rules, in particular around trading, benefit, political activity and reporting.

There is no requirement to register as a charity unless an organisation wishes to be considered charitable - and organisations must be able to prove their public benefit. To become a charity in England and Wales you must apply to the Charity Commission for charitable status if your income is over £5,000 - if your income is below this threshold you can enjoy the benefits of being a charity without registering with the Charity Commission.

More information can be found on the Charity Commission website or *Share*.

Resources

Making wise financial decisions can seem to be fraught with conflicting advice. Here are some of the wide-ranging resources available to help you along the way.

Anglican resources

The Parish Resources website, run by the Church of England National Network of Stewardship Advisors to support and enable those involved with finance and stewardship at parish level, has useful sections on encouraging giving, project funding, how to present your case, writing a business plan and charity law as it affects churches.

Other funding is determined at a Diocesan level - please contact your local diocese for information.

 Parish Resources website
parishresources.org.uk

Church of England Dioceses
churchofengland.org/about-us/dioceses.aspx

Methodist resources

Grants for Methodist projects can be obtained from the circuit, district and connexion.

The 'Resourcing Mission' pages of the Methodist Church website (in the 'Church Life' section or from the A-Z index) have guidance on mission projects and funding.

Further details can be found on page 131.

 Methodist Church of Great Britain
methodistchurch.org.uk

Other resources

CUF Xchange, part of the Church Urban Fund, seeks to promote effective approaches to faith-based social action projects, distinctive practice and how to overcome obstacles.

It has useful sections on funding, project management and community value.

 CUF Xchange
cufx.org.uk

Fundraising for Churches
Jane Grieve, SPCK, 1999,
978-028105058-1

Fresh Expressions resources

The Fresh Expressions website has stories, training, news and further resources covering all aspects of fresh expressions of church.

The Guide has advice on starting, developing and sustaining fresh expressions of church.

Fresh Expressions
freshexpressions.org.uk

The Guide
freshexpressions.org.uk/guide

The Wesley Playhouse

The Howden Clough Project Ltd - known as The Wesley Playhouse - is a church run outreach mission for families providing a soft play area and café. It is a project of Howden Clough Methodist Church, near Birstall. The Wesley Playhouse was formed to spearhead this outreach to offer a new way of being church in a more relevant way in the 21st century. The project is used as the setting for Playhouse Praise on the second Sunday of the month; this includes crafts, songs and Bible stories for all the family.

In June 2005, the Playhouse was successful in obtaining a Biffaward grant of £51,020. Biffaward is a multi-million pound fund which awards grants to community and environmental projects. The fund's money comes from landfill tax credits donated by Biffa Waste Services and it is managed by the Royal Society of Wildlife Trusts on Biffa's behalf.

Through this grant, others began to see that the Playhouse dream could happen. They offered financial support and, over the next few months, more than £90,000 was pledged from individuals and the wider Methodist Church.

The Playhouse's weekly overheads are £800, including running costs and staff wages for a full time church outreach project manager and part time caretaker, cafe manager and catering assistant. It broke even after six months and is now self sufficient thanks to the weekly income received from children's parties and individual customers.

Tubestation

In 2002 a handful of local people recognised that the Methodist School Hall at Polzeath beach, Cornwall, was in danger of disappearing for good. For the next four years they campaigned and fundraised and by 2006 enough finance had been secured to employ an outreach worker for three years, mainly via a Methodist church start-up grant. In October of that year Tubestation was created and match-funding from a second charity doubled the staff to two outreach workers.

The vision quickly outgrew the budget put forward by the Methodist Church, which left just £7,000 for capital spend on development of the premises. It became clear that further fundraising was going to play a major role in the initial set-up phase. A project plan was written and began attracting funding from charities, local government grants and private donors keen to pump-prime an exciting vision which ticked both church and community boxes. The newly refurbished building opened to the public after just nine months - this first phase of development eventually cost £150,000.

One key objective was that the project must aim for self-sufficiency within three years; so the business plan included setting up income streams from the planned new services: internet café; skateboarding; venue hire; art gallery; functions and catering. The team was careful to stimulate community ownership, ensuring they met genuine community needs without duplicating local amenities or treading on toes.

After two years Tubestation registered with the Charity Commission which opened up new funding possibilities, including gift aid. Although the three-year objective to become self-sufficient proved to be unrealistic, the Polzeath project did become self-sustaining at around the four-year mark; including a new team of full-time paid staff who run the café and manage the premises day-to-day.

Tubestation's core mission team however, whose purpose is to continue to develop vision and encourage creative mission in Polzeath and elsewhere in Cornwall's surf culture, continues to rely on grants and donations. Tubestation Polzeath has become so popular that plans are currently being made to develop the site further.

Appendix: Methodist funding for fresh expressions

Grants are available from a number of sources within Methodism for local projects of ministry and mission, including the development of fresh expressions work.

For local churches and circuits, the first source of potential grants is the Circuit Advance Fund (CAF), which allows circuits to draw grants for ministry projects. There is no limit on the amount a circuit can draw as a ministry grant, having taken other committed funds into account and this can be applied for using schedule 16 (approved by the District). This is over and above the £10k p.a. which a circuit can draw using schedule 13a for 'any Methodist purpose'.

The next source of grants is the District Advance Fund (DAF) which receives income from levies on CAFs as well 50% of the net levies received by the Connexional Priority Fund (CPF), making DAFs the primary source for grants for local projects. Enquiries as to how and when to apply for DAF grants should go to your District Chair or Grants Officer.

Beyond District grants, Connexional grants may be available towards fresh expression projects or other ministry and mission projects from a variety of funds. Grants will only normally be for projects which have some Connexional significance (i.e. an impact wider that the local Circuit or District).

Property grants

Grants made from the Fund for Property are totally discretionary. You will need to tell the Resourcing Mission Office why you think the scheme should attract support from this fund - eg. how you have identified the need for the project, how will a grant make a real difference to your scheme.

CPF grants are available to churches that are raising a minimum of £1,000 per member from local effort fundraising towards their project. The calculation for the grant is based on three quarters of the calculation for a Joseph Rank Trust grant, whether or not a grant from The Joseph Rank Trust is being obtained.

The Joseph Rank Trust is a grant-making body entirely independent of the Methodist Church, although applications for should be submitted by The Methodist Property Office or London Committee (churches in the former London districts).

Details of the grant-making criteria for these are available on the Methodist Church website, methodist.org.uk.

External Funding

The Resourcing Mission Office provides information and guidance on external sources of funding for both property and personnel projects. They offer a funding search tailored to your project's location and outcomes. The Active Faith Pack (available on the Methodist Church website) provides a good introduction to finding funding for community projects and gives initial guidance on business plans and applications as well as linking to local sources of advice and information.

Published 2013 by Fresh Expressions
Registered charity #1080103

Copyright © Fresh Expressions 2013
freshexpressions.org.uk

Fresh Expressions, CDO, 1 Hill Top, Coventry, CV1 5AB

Authors: Michael Moynagh (01-07),
John Preston, Andrew Roberts (08)
Series Editor: Karen Carter
Series Designer: Ben Clymo

freshexpressions.org.uk/share/booklets

ISBN 978-0-9568123-0-8

fresh expressions

Related resources

expressions: making a difference
(Fresh Expressions, 2011)

A DVD containing 28 stories illustrating the lessons to be learnt as fresh expressions of church make a difference to people's lives.

fresh! An introduction to fresh expressions of church and pioneer ministry
(SCM Press, 2012)

Practical guidance for starting and sustaining fresh expressions of church in the long term text.

Both available from freshexpressions.org.uk/shop

freshexpressions.org.uk/guide

How-to-do-it advice on starting, developing and sustaining fresh expressions of church.

freshexpressions.org.uk

Further information and stories, training, videos and other resources to download and purchase.